£ 5.99

# Cooking Around The World
# CAJUN

## Cooking Around The World
# CAJUN
### THE VERY BEST OF MODERN LOUISIANA COOKING

**Ruby Le Bois**

LORENZ BOOKS

This edition is published by Lorenz Books

Lorenz Books is an imprint of Anness Publishing Ltd
Hermes House, 88–89 Blackfriars Road, London SE1 8HA
tel. 020 7401 2077; fax 020 7633 9499
www.lorenzbooks.com; info@anness.com

© Anness Publishing Ltd 1994, 2004

UK agent: The Manning Partnership Ltd, 6 The Old Dairy,
Melcombe Road, Bath BA2 3LR;
tel. 01225 478444; fax 01225 478440; sales@manning-partnership.co.uk

UK distributor: Grantham Book Services Ltd, Isaac Newton Way,
Alma Park Industrial Estate, Grantham, Lincs NG31 9SD;
tel. 01476 541080; fax 01476 541061; orders@gbs.tbs-ltd.co.uk

North American agent/distributor: National Book Network,
4501 Forbes Boulevard, Suite 200, Lanham, MD 20706;
tel. 301 459 3366; fax 301 429 5746; www.nbnbooks.com

Australian agent/distributor: Pan Macmillan Australia, Level 18,
St Martins Tower, 31 Market St, Sydney, NSW 2000;
tel. 1300 135 113; fax 1300 135 103; customer.service@macmillan.com.au

New Zealand agent/distributor: David Bateman Ltd, 30 Tarndale Grove,
Off Bush Road, Albany, Auckland;
tel. (09) 415 7664; fax (09) 415 8892

` CIP catalogue record for this book is available from the British Library.

Publisher: Joanna Lorenz
Project Editor: Clare Nicholson
Designer: David Rowley
Photographer: James Duncan
Home Economist: Jane Hartshorn

Previously published as *Cajun & Creole Cuisine*

1 3 5 7 9 10 8 6 4 2

NOTES
.ecipes, quantities are given in both metric and imperial measures and, where
opriate, measures are also given in standard cups and spoons. Follow one set, but
not a mixture, because they are not interchangeable.
Standard spoon and cup measures are level.
1 tsp = 5ml, 1 tbsp = 15ml, 1 cup = 250ml/8fl oz
Australian standard tablespoons are 20ml. Australian readers should use 3 tsp in place
of 1 tbsp for measuring small quantities of gelatine, cornflour, salt, etc.
Medium eggs are used unless otherwise stated.

# Contents

# Introduction

EUROPEANS of aristocratic descent established plantations in Louisiana around the beginning of the seventeenth century, and set about enjoying an elegant life-style with plenty of servants to run their households as well as pick their cotton. For two hundred years the French and Spanish governed Louisiana by turns, and their cooks learned to switch from one cuisine to another, substituting native staples like corn and cayenne for less available wheat and black pepper, and occasionally introducing their own native African ingredients, such as okra, into the cooking pot. It is this mixing of European with indigenous and African culinary traditions that produces the style known as Creole.

American Creole cooking was born and grew up in New Orleans. It was city food, sophisticated and refined to please the palates of the wealthy families for whom it was created. New Orleans prospered and became a centre of wealth-generating commerce: by 1850 half the millionaires in the United States had property around the city.

Those fine gentlemen who set up elegant homes along the Mississippi wanted grand restaurants in which to entertain, and by the turn of the century establishments such as Antoine's were already flourishing. It flourishes still today, joined by a host of others,

*Above   Shellfish is an integral part of cooking in Louisiana.*
*Below   Interior of an Acadian house.*
*Opposite   The blessing of a fishing fleet.*

from the Commander's Palace in the smart Garden District of the city and Lafitte's Landing at Donaldsonville, to Paul Prudhomme's K-Paul's Louisiana Kitchen in the jazzy heart of New Orleans, where the decor is homelier but the food so good a queue for lunch starts forming around 11 am. (K-Paul's takes no bookings).

Cajun cooking, although also French-based, is a hearty, agrarian style of quite different pedigree. The word Cajun is a corruption of the prettier "Acadian", and the first Acadia was in Nova Scotia, peopled from 1620 by

French peasant farmers and fishermen. They brought their own culinary traditions with them from France, but adapted them to a new and unfamiliar set of ingredients. Then in the mid-eighteenth century these Roman Catholic Acadians found themselves once more displaced, this time exiled by British colonialists.

Communities and families were split up as men were first shipped out in one direction, then women and children herded off in another. Eventually a number found their way to "the French triangle" of South-West Louisiana, and once more hooked their big black iron cooking pots over their fires and looked around their new Acadia for something to put in them. There was plenty for those who knew where to look, and these first Cajuns, whose forefathers had already proved their survival skills in an unfamiliar environment, again set about adapting their culinary technique to a new set of ingredients.

For those near the coast there was seafood aplenty, while further inland the bayous were teeming with sweet-water fish including the crawfish that is still a signature of Cajun cooking. There was big game – bear as well as deer – and plenty of wild fowl. There were wild vegetables, herbs and fruits to be gathered, and native Americans to teach them where to find them and how best to use them, sensing no threat from these hard-working peasant settlers. By the middle of this century these two cuisines, the Cajun and the Creole, both born on American soil of European ancestry, had begun to merge, at least in the minds of the increasing stream of visiting pilgrims to the birthplace of jazz. Maybe you could tell Cajun cooking from Creole at the home hearth, but in the restaurants where visitors ate, distinctions became blurred.

In the decades that followed the jet-powered explosion of tourism, full-

*Above  The Pontalba Apartments in New Orleans' French Quarter were built in 1850 and are believed to be the oldest apartment buildings in America.*

blooded Cajun cooks like Paul Prudhomme joined the restaurant boom, and found it necessary to adapt the long, slow cooking of their mothers to fit the demands on a restaurant kitchen. Faster heat meant shorter cooking times, a principle that reached its apotheosis in the blackening technique; blackened redfish, considered by many visitors the foundation stone of Cajun cooking, was a dish invented by Prudhomme in 1979. In 1983 Paul Prudhomme cooked for visiting heads of state at Ronald Reagan's 1983 Williamsburg summit, and Cajun cuisine was launched in its worldwide boom.

While international marketing was doing its inevitable bit to corrupt Cajun cooking to fit the new hot culinary fashion, Prudhomme and his contem

# Roux

Roux is a crucial ingredient in many Cajun and Creole dishes. It is a thickener and a flavouring agent, and it needs to be cooked slowly and with constant attention. Heat the oil in a big saucepan, when it is hot, add the flour and stir constantly with a wooden spoon or whisk until it reaches the desired colour. It is vital to stir constantly to darken the roux without burning. Should black specks occur at any stage of cooking, you must discard the roux and start it again.

*Top Left  Light Brown*
*Top Right  Peanut Butter Brown*
*Bottom Left  Dark Nutty Brown*
*Bottom Right  Black*

*Left  Freshness is everything when it comes to cooking with vegetables.*

poraries were at their stoves evolving a new, authentic Louisiana cooking that married the old styles of Cajun and Creole, while taking advantage of ingredients made available by jet-set freighting and the new interstate highways already criss-crossing the bayous. This New Louisiana cooking is a true descendant of the American–European heritage, its hallmark exciting but judicious pepper-spicing, using Old World black and white peppercorns as well as the huge native American range of red capsicum, and emphasizing always the freshness of available ingredients.

One of the exponents of the New Louisiana style, John Folse, chef at Lafitte's Landing restaurant, explained on a visit to London, where he cooked for food and travel writers, that the heredity of the cuisine was entirely based on adaptation. What is one person's trash food is another's luxury. The first Cajun settlers found the shoreline awash with oysters and lobsters, so that is what they used. If they had found mussels they would undoubtedly have used those. It's a happy-go-lucky, permissive message to give to cooks who want the adventure of Louisiana food: go ahead, use what's around you. Just make sure it's good and fresh, and cook it with love.

# Starters, Snacks & Sauces

*All the ingredients for appetizing starters, snacks and sauces are abundant in Louisiana – seafood in vast quantity and variety, sweet peppers to grill to velvet smoothness, as well as the hot variety to fire up appetites, splendid salad greens, luscious tomatoes and golden sweetcorn. Many of the vegetable dishes of the area are shown off best in the stand-alone status of starter or light meal, perhaps with a salad garnish, as in the case of Hot Parsnip Fritters and Creole Cheese Potato Puffs, or in combination with each other like Sweetcorn Cakes with Grilled Tomatoes. These are the sort of dishes to set the Louisiana style of a meal, and indeed they are even setting the standards for a new style of dining in Cajun country.*

# Beignets

*In New Orleans where a night on the town really can last all night, revellers are glad of a pit-stop at the Café du Monde, which serves its favourite treats of 'café au lait' and sugary beignets 24 hours a day. Chef John False of Lafitte's Landing restaurant, who is deeply interested in Louisiana history, says the recipe was brought to Louisiana in 1727 by Ursuline nuns. This is his version of their recipe.*

**MAKES 20**

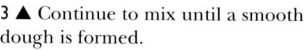

INGREDIENTS
*1 packet dried yeast*
*400 g/14 oz/3½ cups plain flour*
*1 tsp salt*
*50 g/2 oz/1¼ cup caster sugar*
*300 ml/10 fl oz/1¼ cups milk*
*3 eggs, beaten*
*25 g/1 oz/2 tbsp butter, melted*
*oil for deep-frying*
*115 g/4 oz/1 cup icing sugar*

I Dissolve the yeast in 4 tbsp warm water and set aside.

2 ▲ In a large mixing bowl, combine the flour, salt and caster sugar and mix well. Fold in the dissolved yeast, milk, eggs and melted butter.

3 ▲ Continue to mix until a smooth dough is formed.

4 Knead the dough until smooth and elastic. Cover the dough with a towel and leave to rise in a warm place for 1 hour.

5 ▲ Roll out the dough to 5 mm/¼ in thick on a well-floured surface. Cut into rectangular shapes about 5 × 7.5 cm/ 2 × 3 in and put them in a lightly floured Swiss roll tin.

6 Cover with a towel and leave to rise in a warm place for an hour or until they have doubled their size.

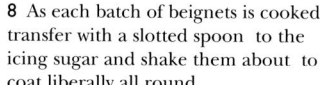

7 ▲ Put the icing sugar into a deep dish or oven tin. Heat the oil for deep-frying and fry the beignets in batches, turning each, until golden brown on both sides. Drain well on kitchen paper.

8 As each batch of beignets is cooked, transfer with a slotted spoon to the icing sugar and shake them about to coat liberally all round.

**COOK'S TIP**

*The important thing with beignets, as with all doughnuts, is to have the oil at the right temperature to cook the dough right through to the middle before the outside is too dark brown.*

*Treat the first beignet or two as a test. Break them open and if they are still sticky in the middle lower the heat and allow the oil to cool down a bit before continuing with the next batch.*

*Eat the beignets soon after cooking, and certainly on the same day as they are made.*

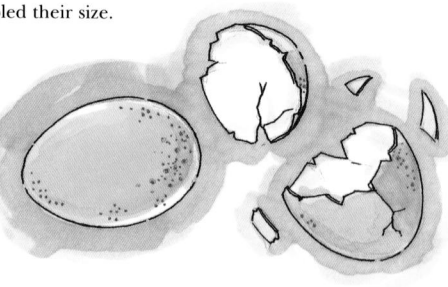

# Creole Omelette

**SERVES 3–4**

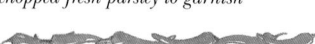

INGREDIENTS

*1 large Spanish onion, finely chopped*
*25 g/1 oz/2 tbsp butter*
*1 garlic clove, crushed*
*2 tbsp soft white breadcrumbs*
*4 large tomatoes, skinned and chopped*
*50 g/2 oz/½ cup lean cooked ham*
  *finely chopped*
*salt, freshly ground black pepper and*
  *cayenne*
*6 eggs, lightly beaten*
*chopped fresh parsley to garnish*

1  Soften the onion in the butter in a heavy frying pan, stirring regularly over a low heat for about 10 minutes.

2 ▲ Add the garlic and breadcrumbs and continue to stir over the heat until the breadcrumbs begin to crisp.

3 ▲ Add the tomatoes and cook for 10–15 minutes until they have broken down. Stir in the ham and season the mixture quite highly to compensate for the eggs.

4 ▲ Preheat the grill. Stir the beaten eggs through the mixture and continue to stir over the heat, breaking up the base as it sets to allow the uncooked mixture through.

5  When the omelette begins to set, leave it over a low heat until it is almost completely set.

6  Finish the omelette under the grill to cook the top. Serve either turned out onto a warm serving plate or straight from the pan, cut in wedges. Garnish with chopped parsley.

## COOK'S TIP

*You can leave out the ham to make the omelette suitable for vegetarians. Or, you can replace the ham with cut-up spicy sausages.*

# Muffuletto Sandwich

*In New Orleans you buy your Muffuletto sandwich ready-made from one of the grocery stores on Chartres Street that are famous for it, and where they also make up the olive pickle (an essential ingredient) by the barrel-load. There it comes in a special 25 cm/10 in diameter soft loaf, like an extra large hamburger bun, served in quarters. You can make it in a French loaf.*

**SERVES 4**

INGREDIENTS
**For the olive pickle**
*1 celery stick, finely chopped*
*1 garlic clove, crushed*
*1 canned sweet red pepper, drained and finely chopped*
*75 g/3 oz/⅔ cup stoned green olives, chopped*
*2 tbsp pickled cocktail onions, drained and coarsely chopped*
*2 tsp capers, drained and halved*
*3 tbsp olive oil*
*2 tsp red wine vinegar*

**For the sandwich**
*1 large French loaf*
*4 thin slices Parma ham*
*50 g/2 oz Provolone or Emmental cheese, thinly sliced*
*black pepper*
*50 g/2 oz Italian salami, rinded and thinly sliced*

I ▲ Mix all the vegetable and pickled ingredients for the olive pickle, then stir in the oil and vinegar and refrigerate.

2 ▲ To make the sandwich, halve the loaf and cut it lengthways. Line the base with Parma ham. Lay the cheese on top and grind on some black pepper, then overlay with slices of salami.

3 ▲ Finally spoon the olive pickle on top of the salami and press the sandwich shut.

# Eggs Sardou

*Restaurants don't come and go much in New Orleans: Antoine's, where this dish was created in 1908, is still there, right in the heart of jazzland. The dish's popularity has spread and it now crops up on brunch menus as well as being a favourite starter.*

**SERVES 4**

INGREDIENTS
*4 large artichokes*
*500 g/1¼ lb raw spinach*
*50 g/2 oz/4 tbsp butter*
*2 tbsp plain flour*
*175 ml/6 fl oz/¾ cup milk*
*4 canned anchovy fillets, drained and mashed*
*salt, freshly ground black pepper, grated nutmeg and Tabasco sauce*
*4 eggs*

**For the Hollandaise sauce**
*2 tbsp white wine vinegar*
*4 black peppercorns*
*1 bay leaf*
*2 egg yolks, at room temperature*
*115 g/4 oz/½ cup butter, at warm room temperature, cubed*
*salt and freshly ground black pepper*

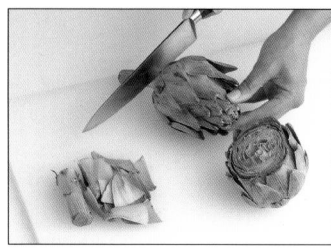

**1 ▲** With a sharp knife, cut the stems from the artichokes, then cut off the top half of each artichoke and scoop out the centre. Set aside.

**2 ▲** Wash the spinach thoroughly, trimming off any discoloured bits and the coarser stems. Put the spinach into a deep pan with just the water that clings to it. Cover and cook until it wilts right down. Turn out into a colander and, when it's cool enough to handle, squeeze out much of the moisture. Slice across the ball of spinach both ways to chop it.

**3** To make the Hollandaise sauce, boil the vinegar with 2 tsp water, the peppercorns and bay leaf in a small pan until the liquid is reduced to 1 tbsp. Leave to cool.

**4 ▲** Cream the egg yolks with one cube of soft butter and a pinch of salt in a heatproof bowl, then strain on the vinegar, set the bowl over a pan of boiling water and turn off the heat.

**5** Whisk in the remaining butter a cube at a time, adding each cube as the one before melts into the sauce. Carry on whisking until the sauce is shiny and thick. Season with salt and pepper. Leave over the pan of water to keep warm.

**6 ▲** Bring a wide pan full of salted water to the boil. Add the artichokes, cover and cook for about 30 minutes or until tender. Lift them with a slotted spoon onto warmed serving plates and keep warm.

**7 ▲** Meanwhile, to finish the spinach, melt the butter in a wide pan, mix in the flour and stir for 1 minute over the heat until the roux froths and bubbles. Take off the heat and pour in the milk gradually, stirring constantly. When the sauce loosens, return it to the heat and continue stirring in the milk.

**8** When the sauce reaches simmering point, stir in the mashed anchovies and leave to simmer for about 5 minutes. Then add the chopped spinach, return to simmering point, season with black pepper, nutmeg, Tabasco sauce and salt if it needs it, and keep warm.

**9** Poach the eggs 2 at a time in the pan of artichoke cooking water.

**10** To assemble the dish, spoon some spinach into each artichoke, allowing it to spill over the edges. Set a poached egg on the plate and spoon Hollandaise sauce over.

# Cream of Red Pepper Soup

*Grilling peppers gives them a smoky sweetness that's delicious in salads or, as here, in a velvety soup with a secret flavouring of rosemary to add resinous depth. The soup is equally good served hot or chilled.*

**SERVES 4**

INGREDIENTS
*4 sweet red peppers*
*1 onion, finely chopped*
*25 g/1 oz/2 tbsp butter*
*1 sprig fresh rosemary*
*1.2 litres/2 pints/5 cups chicken or light*
    *vegetable stock*
*3 tbsp tomato purée*
*120 ml/4 fl oz/½ cup double cream*
*salt, freshly ground black pepper and*
    *paprika*

**COOK'S TIP**

*Use vegetable rather than chicken stock to make the soup suitable for vegetarians.*

1 ▲ Preheat the grill. Put the peppers in the grill pan under the grill and turn them regularly until the skins have blackened all round. Put them into polythene bags, sealing them closed. Leave them for 20 minutes.

2 ▲ Flake the blackened skin off the peppers, avoiding rinsing them under the tap if possible as this loses some of the natural oil and hence the flavour.

3 Halve the peppers, removing the seeds, stalks and pith, then roughly chop the flesh.

4 Melt the butter in a deep saucepan. Add the onion and rosemary and cook gently over a low heat for about 5 minutes. Remove the rosemary and discard.

5 Add the peppers and stock to the onion, bring to the boil and simmer for 15 minutes. Stir in the tomato purée, then process or sieve the soup to a smooth purée.

6 ▲ Stir in half the cream and season with salt, if necessary, with pepper and a little paprika.

7 Serve the soup hot or chilled, with the remaining cream swirled delicately on top. Speckle the cream very lightly with a pinch of paprika

# Creole Onion Soup

**SERVES 4**

### INGREDIENTS
*50 g/2 oz/4 tbsp butter*
*2 large onions, quartered and thinly sliced*
*1 bay leaf*
*3 tbsp plain flour*
*1 litre/1¾ pints/4½ cups chicken stock*
*75 g/3 oz/¾ cup grated Cheddar cheese*
*2 tbsp bourbon*
*120 ml/4 fl oz/½ cup milk*
*salt and freshly ground black pepper*

4 Add the bourbon, return to the boil, cook for 1 minute, then stir in the milk. Return once more to simmering point, remove the bay leaf, correct the seasoning with salt if necessary and plenty of black pepper.

5 Ladle the soup into bowls and scatter each with a little of the remaining grated Cheddar.

3 ▲ Gradually stir in the remaining stock, bring to the boil, partially cover and simmer for 20 minutes.

I ▲ Melt the butter in a deep saucepan, add the onions and bay leaf and cook over a very low heat for about 20 minutes until the onions are very soft and mushy, but not darkened beyond pale gold.

2 ▲ Sprinkle on the flour, stir over the same low heat until it is well amalgamated, then lift the pan off the heat and stir in 250 ml/8 fl oz/1 cup of the stock, a little at a time. Return to the heat and stir until it thickens smoothly. Add 50 g/2 oz/½ cup of the cheese and continue stirring gently until it melts.

# Hot Parsnip Fritters on Baby Spinach

*Fritters are a natural favourite of Cajun cooks, with their love for deep-frying. The technique brings out the luscious sweetness of parsnips, here set, none too traditionally, on a walnut-dressed salad of baby spinach leaves.*

**SERVES 4**

INGREDIENTS
*2 large parsnips*
*1 egg, separated*
*115 g/4 oz/1 cup plain flour*
*120 ml/4 fl oz/½ cup milk*
*salt, freshly ground black pepper and*
*    cayenne*
*115 g/4 oz baby spinach leaves*
*2 tbsp olive oil*
*1 tbsp walnut oil*
*1 tbsp sherry vinegar*
*oil for deep-frying*
*1 tbsp coarsely chopped walnuts*

I ▲ Peel the parsnips, bring to the boil in a pan of salted water and simmer for 10–15 minutes until tender but not in the least mushy. Drain, cool and cut diagonally into slices about 5 cm/2 in long × 5 mm–1 cm/¼–½ in thick.

2  Put the egg yolk into a well in the flour in a bowl and mix in with a fork, gradually pulling in the surrounding flour. Begin adding the milk, while continuing to mix in the flour. Season with salt, and black and cayenne peppers, and beat with a whisk until the batter is smooth.

3  Wash and dry the spinach leaves and put them in a bowl. In a screwtop jar, mix the olive and walnut oils, sherry vinegar, salt and pepper.

4 ▲ When you are ready to serve, whisk the egg white to the soft-peak stage, fold in a little of the yolk batter, then fold the white into the batter. Heat the oil for frying.

5  Meanwhile, shake the dressing jar vigorously, then toss the salad in the dressing. Arrange the dressed leaves on 4 salad plates and scatter with walnuts.

6 ▲ Dip the parsnip slices in batter and fry a few at a time until puffy and golden. Drain on kitchen paper and keep warm. To serve, arrange the fritters on top of the salad leaves.

# Eggs in Remoulade Sauce

*There are as many recipes for
Remoulade sauce as there are cooks in
Louisiana. This one comes from the
McIlhenny family, makers of Tabasco
sauce. Naturally they splash some of the
hot stuff into their Remoulade.*

**SERVES 4**

INGREDIENTS
*3 tbsp coarse-ground mustard
2 tsp paprika
1 tsp Tabasco sauce
1 tsp salt
½ tsp freshly ground black pepper
3 tbsp tarragon vinegar
250 ml/8 fl oz/1 cup olive oil
3 spring onions, shredded
1 celery stick, shredded
3 tbsp finely chopped fresh parsley
6 hard-boiled eggs
mustard and cress to garnish*

l  Whisk together the mustard,
paprika, Tabasco sauce, salt and
pepper, then beat in the vinegar.

**2 ▲** Beating constantly, add the oil in a
slow thin trickle, continuing to beat
until the sauce is thick and smooth.

**COOK'S TIP**

*This is an easy dish to make in a larger
quantity for a buffet table. Leave the final
assembly as late as you can before serving.*

**3 ▲** Stir in the spring onions, celery
and parsley and mix well.

**4 ▲** Cover the bowl and leave to stand
for at least 2 hours to allow the flavours
to blend. Meanwhile, shell the eggs and
halve them lengthways. Arrange 3
halves on each of 4 side plates. Spoon
the sauce over, then sprinkle lightly
with mustard and cress.

# Sweetcorn Cakes with Grilled Tomatoes

**SERVES 4**

INGREDIENTS
*1 large cob sweetcorn*
*75 g/3 oz/³/4 cup plain flour*
*1 egg*
*a little milk*
*salt and freshly ground black pepper*
*2 large firm tomatoes*
*1 garlic clove*
*1 tsp dried oregano*
*2–3 tbsp oil, plus extra for shallow-frying*
*8 cupped leaves iceberg lettuce*
*shredded fresh basil leaves to garnish*

1 ▲ Pull the husks and silk away from the corn, then hold the cob upright on a board and cut downwards with a heavy knife to strip off the kernels. Put them into a pan of boiling water and cook for 3 minutes after the water has returned to the boil, then drain and rinse under the cold tap to cool quickly.

2 Put the flour into a bowl and break the egg into a well in the middle, then start stirring in the flour with a fork, adding a little milk to make a soft dropping consistency. Stir in the drained corn and season.

3 ▲ Preheat the grill. Halve the tomatoes horizontally and make 2 or 3 criss-cross slashes across the cut side of each half. Crush the garlic and rub it, the oregano and some salt and pepper over the cut surface of each half, then trickle with oil and grill until lightly browned.

4 ▲ While the tomatoes grill, heat some oil in a wide frying pan and drop a tablespoon of batter into the centre. Cook, one at a time, over a low heat and turn as soon as the top is set. Drain on kitchen paper and keep warm while cooking remaining fritters. The mixture should make at least 8 corn cakes.

5 Put 2 corn cakes onto lettuce leaves, garnish with basil and serve with a grilled tomato half.

# Green Herb Gumbo

*Traditionally served at the end of Lent, this is a joyful, sweetly spiced and revitalizing dish, even if you haven't been fasting. The variety of green ingredients is important, so buy substitutes if you cannot find all of them.*

**SERVES 6–8**

INGREDIENTS
*350 g/12 oz piece raw smoked gammon*
*2 tbsp lard or cooking oil*
*1 large Spanish onion, roughly chopped*
*2–3 garlic cloves, crushed*
*1 tsp dried oregano*
*1 tsp dried thyme*
*2 bay leaves*
*2 cloves*
*2 celery sticks, finely sliced*
*1 sweet green pepper, seeded and chopped*
*½ medium green cabbage, stalked and finely shredded*
*2 litres/3½ pints/9 cups light stock or water*
*200 g/7 oz spring greens or kale, finely shredded*
*200 g/7 oz Chinese mustard cabbage, finely shredded (see Cook's Tip)*
*200 g/7 oz spinach, shredded*
*1 bunch watercress, shredded*
*6 spring onions, finely shredded*
*25 g/1 oz/½ cup chopped fresh parsley*
*½ tsp ground allspice*
*¼ nutmeg, grated*
*salt, freshly ground black pepper and cayenne*
*hot French bread or garlic bread to serve*

**COOK'S TIP**

*Chinese mustard greens are increasingly available in supermarkets, as well as from oriental shops and markets. If, however, you can't find them, substitute turnip tops or kohlrabi leaves.*

1 ▲ Dice the ham quite small, keeping any fat and rind in one separate piece. Put the fat piece with the lard or oil into a deep saucepan and heat until it sizzles. Stir in the diced ham, onion, garlic, oregano and thyme and stir over a medium heat for 5 minutes.

2 Add the bay leaves, cloves, celery and sweet green pepper and stir for another 2–3 minutes over the heat, then add the cabbage and stock or water. Bring to the boil and simmer for 5 minutes.

3 ▲ Add the spring greens or kale and mustard cabbage, boil for a further 2 minutes, then add the spinach, watercress and spring onions and lower the heat. Simmer for 1 minute after it returns to the boil, then add the parsley, ground allspice and nutmeg, salt, black pepper and cayenne to taste.

4 Remove the piece of ham fat and, if you can find them, the cloves. Serve immediately, with hot French bread or garlic bread.

# Corn and Crab Bisque

*A Louisiana classic, and certainly
luxurious enough for a dinner party,
which makes it worth the trouble. The
crab shells together with the corn cobs,
from which the kernels are stripped,
make a fine-flavoured stock.*

**SERVES 8**

INGREDIENTS
*4 large cobs sweetcorn*
*2 bay leaves*
*salt, freshly ground black and white*
 *pepper, and cayenne*
*1 cooked crab weighing about 1 kg/2¼ lb*
*25 g/1 oz/2 tbsp butter*
*2 tbsp plain flour*
*300 ml/10 fl oz/1¼ cups whipping cream*
*6 spring onions, shredded*
*hot French bread or grissini bread sticks*
 *to serve*

I Pull away the husks and silk from the
cobs of corn and strip off the kernels
(see step 1 of Sweetcorn Cakes with
Grilled Tomatoes, for the method).

2 Keep the kernels on one side and put
the stripped cobs into a deep saucepan
or flameproof casserole with 3 litres/
5 pints/12½ cups cold water, the bay
leaves and 2 tsp salt. Bring to the boil
and leave to simmer while you prepare
the crab.

3 ▲ Pull away the two flaps between
the big claws of the crab, stand it on its
'nose' where the flaps were and bang
down firmly with the heel of your hand
on the rounded end.

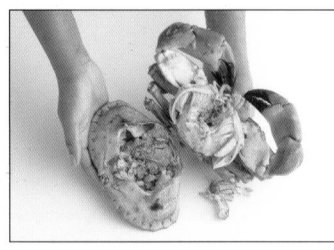

4 ▲ Separate the crab from its top
shell, keeping the shell.

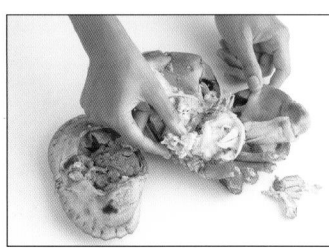

5 ▲ Push out the crab's mouth and its
abdominal sac immediately below the
mouth, and discard.

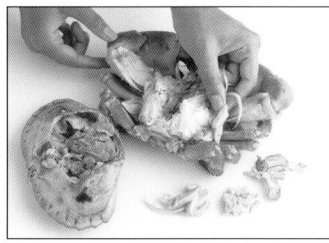

6 ▲ Pull away the feathery gills
surrounding the central chamber and
discard. Scrape out all the semi-liquid
brown meat from the shell and keep it.

7 ▲ Crack the claws in as many places
as necessary to extract all the white
meat. Pick out the white meat from the
fragile cavities in the central body of the
crab. Set aside all the crabmeat, brown
and white. Put the spidery legs, back
shell and all the other pieces of shell
into the pan with the corn cobs. Simmer
for a further 15 minutes, then strain
the stock into a clean pan and boil hard
to reduce to 2 litres/3½ pints/9 cups.

8 Meanwhile melt the butter in a small
pan and sprinkle in the flour. Stir
constantly over a low heat until the
roux is the colour of rich cream (see
Introduction).

9 Off the heat, slowly stir in 250 ml/
8 fl oz/1 cup of the stock. Return to the
heat and stir until it thickens, then stir
this thickened mixture into the pot of
strained stock.

10 Add the corn kernels, return to the
boil and simmer for 5 minutes.

11 Add the crabmeat, cream and
spring onions and season with salt,
black or white pepper (or a bit of both)
and cayenne. Return to the boil and
simmer for a further 2 minutes. Serve
with hot French bread or grissini
bread sticks.

**COOK'S TIP**

*You can, if you prefer, ask your fish-
monger to remove all the inedible bits of
the crab – the mouth, stomach sac and gills.*

# Prawn and Artichoke Salad

*Artichokes are a very popular Louisiana ingredient – and the local cooks use canned hearts in the best of circles.*

**SERVES 4**

INGREDIENTS
*1 garlic clove*
*salt and freshly ground black pepper*
*2 tsp Dijon mustard*
*4 tbsp red wine vinegar*
*150 ml/5 fl oz/²⁄₃ cup olive oil*
*3 tbsp shredded fresh basil leaves or 2 tbsp*
*    finely chopped fresh parsley*
*1 red onion, very finely sliced*
*350 g/12 oz cooked shelled prawns*
*400 g/14 oz can artichoke hearts*
*½ head iceberg lettuce*

1 ▲ Chop the garlic, then crush it to a pulp with 1 tsp salt, using the flat of a heavy knife blade.

2 ▲ Mix the garlic and mustard to a paste, then beat in the vinegar and finally the olive oil, beating hard to make a thick creamy dressing. Season with black pepper and, if necessary, additional salt.

3 Stir the basil or parsley into the dressing, followed by the sliced onion. Leave to stand for 30 minutes at room temperature, then stir in the prawns and refrigerate for 1 hour or until ready to serve.

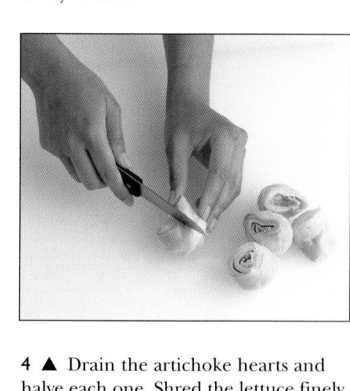

4 ▲ Drain the artichoke hearts and halve each one. Shred the lettuce finely.

5 Make a bed of lettuce on a serving platter or 4 individual salad plates and spread the artichoke hearts over it.

6 Immediately before serving, pour the prawns and onion and their marinade over the top of the salad.

# Creole Cheese Potato Puffs

*It's worth boiling extra potatoes just to have some left over to mash for this heartening starter.*

**SERVES 4–6**

INGREDIENTS
*3 tbsp milk*
*25 g/1 oz/2 tbsp butter*
*450 g/1 lb/2½ cups cold mashed potatoes*
*50 g/2 oz/½ cup grated Cheddar cheese*
*4 spring onions, shredded*
*salt, freshly ground black pepper and grated nutmeg*
*2 eggs, separated*
*watercress and cherry tomatoes to garnish*

1 Preheat the oven to 220°C/425°F/ Gas 7 and generously butter a 12-hole non-stick bun sheet, buttering the sections between the indents as well.

2 ▲ Warm the milk and butter to just below boiling point in a small pan, then mix thoroughly into the mashed potatoes with the cheese, spring onions and seasoning. Mix in the egg yolks and beat thoroughly.

**COOK'S TIP**

*Garnished elegantly, these puffs make a pretty starter, but on a more homely occasion they are just as good served with sausages and tomato ketchup.*

3 ▲ Whisk the egg whites to soft peaks. Mix a tablespoon or two of the whites thoroughly into the potato mixture to loosen it, then fold the rest of the whites through the potato as lightly as you can.

4 ▲ Spoon the mixture into the bun tins and bake in the oven for about 15 minutes, until the puffs have risen and are tinged golden brown. Serve immediately, garnished with watercress and cherry tomatoes.

# Red Pepper Jelly

*A sweet-savoury jelly that's good with pork, lamb and duck. Serve it at the table to spoon out alongside the meat, or use it as a glaze for grilled cuts (see the recipe for Duck Breasts with Red Pepper Jelly glaze). It's also good with a sharp cheese such as Cheddar.*

**MAKES ABOUT 1.5 kg/3 lb**

INGREDIENTS
*1 kg/2¼ lb eating apples
juice of 1 lemon
1 kg/2¼ lb/5 cups granulated sugar
115 g/4 oz red chilli peppers, seeded and
    roughly chopped
1 large sweet red pepper, seeded and
    roughly chopped
1 large Spanish onion, chopped
350 ml/12 fl oz/1½ cups cider vinegar*

1 ▲ Cut each apple into about 8 pieces, discarding only the bruised and damaged sections, not the cores, peel, seeds or stems. Put into a deep saucepan with the lemon juice and 1 litre/1¾ pints/ 4½ cups cold water. Bring to the boil, cover and simmer for 30 minutes.

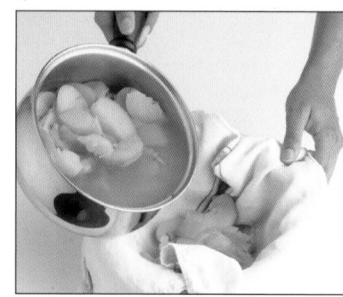

2 ▲ Line a colander with a clean tea towel and set it over a deep bowl. Pour the apples and liquid into this and leave to drop through undisturbed.

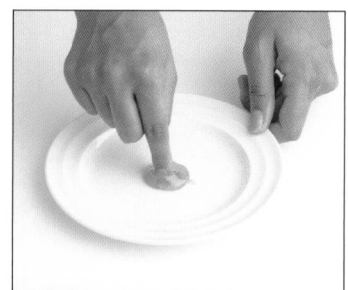

3 ▲ Discard the apple debris and pour the liquid into a saucepan with 800 g/ 1¾ lb/4 cups of the sugar. Stir over a low heat until the sugar dissolves completely and the liquid clears. Raise the heat and boil without further stirring until a little of the syrup, spread on a cold plate, wrinkles when you push it with your finger. Start testing after 15 minutes, but anticipate that it may take 30 minutes.

4 ▲ Either mince or process the red chilli peppers, sweet red peppers and onion together to create a fine hash.

5 Stir the vegetables, vinegar and remaining sugar together in a large saucepan over a low heat until the sugar dissolves. Raise the heat as boiling point approaches and boil for 5 minutes, then add to the apple syrup and once again boil until the mixture passes the wrinkle test.

6 ▲ Ladle the jelly into hot sterilized jars, cover with vinegar-proof discs and lids and cool for about 20 minutes, then invert the jars to redistribute the flecks of pepper. After a further 20 minutes turn them the right way up to complete cooling. Wipe away any external stickiness with a hot damp cloth, then label. Store in a cool place. The jelly should keep for up to 1 year.

# Cajun Bloody Mary

*It was in New York that the life-enhancing dash of Tabasco was first added to the classic morning-after reviver. In Cajun country they make their Bloody Marys by the pitcherful.*

**SERVES 6**

INGREDIENTS
*250 ml/8 fl oz/1 cup vodka*
*2 tbsp fresh lime juice*
*1 tbsp Worcestershire sauce*
*1 litre/1¾ pints/4½ cups tomato juice,*
   *chilled*
*celery salt and black pepper*
*4–6 dashes Tabasco sauce*
*ice cubes and celery sticks to serve*

1 ▲ Mix the vodka, lime juice and Worcestershire sauce thoroughly in a measuring jug, then mix into the chilled tomato juice in a pitcher.

2  Season to taste with celery salt, black pepper and Tabasco sauce and stir very thoroughly with a long spoon.

3  Pour over ice cubes in chunky tumblers and serve with a celery stick, preferably with a bit of greenery attached, as a stirrer, in each glass.

# Avery Island Salsa

*Tabasco sauce is made, as it has been for over a century, by the McIlhenny family on Avery Island off the coast of Louisiana. The present generation of McIlhennys has concocted a thick and spicy salsa, which keeps up to five days in the fridge. But be warned – they like it hot on Avery Island. Cut down on the Tabasco for a milder salsa. This is great with all grilled food, and even better with barbecued.*

**MAKES 600 ml/1 pint/2½ cups**

INGREDIENTS
*2 tbsp olive oil*
*1 large onion, coarsely chopped*
*2 sweet green peppers, seeded and diced*
*2 × 400 g/14 oz cans chopped tomatoes*
*1 tbsp fresh lime juice*
*2 tsp Tabasco sauce*
*½ tsp salt*
*2 tbsp chopped fresh coriander leaves*

1 ▲ Heat the oil in a heavy saucepan. Add the onion and peppers and sauté for 5–6 minutes, stirring frequently.

2  Add the tomatoes, stir and bring to the boil. Reduce the heat and simmer for 6–8 minutes until the salsa thickens a bit. Remove from heat, stir in the lime juice, Tabasco sauce and salt, then cool.

3 ▲ Stir the chopped coriander leaves through the cooled salsa and pot in clean jars. Cover and refrigerate.

*Cajun Bloody Mary (top) and Avery Island Salsa (bottom).*

# Fish & Seafood

*Louisiana is a low-lying and wet state with a long coastline along the Gulf of Mexico, so there's no shortage of fish and seafood, both from the fresh waters of the bayous and rivers and from the sea. But much of what is commonplace in fishmarkets there – oysters, soft-shell crab, redfish and crawfish – are either hugely expensive or completely unknown outside the region. With fish, however, more than with any other foodstuff, substitution is acceptable, and unless an expensive ingredient is essential to the finished dish, I have recommended cheaper and more available fish.*

# Louisiana Seafood Gumbo

*Gumbo is a soup, but is served over rice as a main course. This recipe is based on a gumbo that chef John Folse, of the renowned Louisiana restaurant Lafitte's Landing, served on a visit to London. In his neck of the bayous, where they are cheap and prolific, oysters are an important ingredient. However, his suggestion to substitute mussels for oysters, works very well too.*

**SERVES 6**

INGREDIENTS
*450 g/1 lb mussels*
*450 g/1 lb prawns*
*1 cooked crab weighing about 1 kg/2¼ lb*
*salt*
*1 small bunch of parsley, leaves chopped*
   *and stalks reserved*
*150 ml/5 fl oz/⅔ cup cooking oil*
*115 g/4 oz/1 cup plain flour*
*1 sweet green pepper, seeded and chopped*
*1 large onion, chopped*
*2 celery sticks, sliced*
*3 garlic cloves, finely chopped*
*75 g/3 oz smoked spiced sausage, skinned*
   *and sliced*
*6 spring onions, shredded*
*cayenne*
*Tabasco sauce*
*boiled American long-grain rice to serve*

I ▲ Wash the mussels in several changes of cold water, scrubbing away any barnacles and pulling off the black 'beards' that protrude between the shells. Discard any mussels that are broken or any open ones that don't close when you tap them firmly.

2 ▲ Heat 250 ml/8 fl oz/1 cup water in a deep saucepan and, when it boils, add the mussels, cover tightly and cook over a high heat, shaking regularly, for 3 minutes. As the mussels open, lift them out with tongs into a sieve set over a bowl. Discard any that refuse to open after a further 1 minute's cooking.

3 ▲ Shell the mussels, discarding the shells. Return the liquor from the bowl to the pan and make the quantity up to 2 litres/3½ pints/9 cups with water.

4 Shell the prawns and put the shells and heads into the saucepan.

5 Remove all the meat from the crab (see the Corn and Crab Bisque recipe), separating the brown and white meat. Add all the pieces of shell to the saucepan with 2 tsp salt.

6 Bring the shellfish stock to the boil, skimming regularly to remove the froth that rises as boiling point approaches.

7 When no more froth rises from the shellfish stock, add the parsley stalks and simmer for 15 minutes. Cool the stock, then strain off the liquor, discarding all the solids. Make up to 2 litres/3½ pints/9 cups with water.

8 Make a roux with the oil and flour (see Introduction). Stir constantly over the heat with a wooden spoon or whisk until it reaches a golden-brown colour. It is vital to stir constantly to darken the roux without burning. Should black specks occur at any stage of cooking, discard the roux and start again.

9 ▲ As soon as the roux is the right colour, add the pepper, onion, celery and garlic and continue cooking until they are soft – about 3 minutes. Then add the sausage. Reheat the stock.

10 Stir the brown crabmeat into the roux, then ladle in the hot stock a little at a time, stirring constantly until it is all smoothly incorporated. Bring to a low boil and simmer the soup for 30 minutes, partially covered.

11 Add the prawns, mussels, white crabmeat and spring onions. Return to the boil, season with salt if necessary, cayenne and a dash or two of Tabasco sauce, and simmer for a further minute.

12 Add the chopped parsley leaves and serve immediately, ladling the soup over the hot rice in soup plates.

**COOK'S TIP**

*It's important to have the onion, green pepper and celery prepared and ready to add to the roux the minute it reaches the correct golden-brown stage, as this arrests its darkening.*

# Blackened Redfish

*Paul Prudhomme, inventor of this dish, recommends it be cooked out of doors over a Butane flame. Since this is not practical for most cooks, there are a few precautions to be taken for more conventional cooking.*

*First, don't attempt it in a kitchen you can't ventilate, for this fierce cooking method produces plenty of smoke: open the windows, turn on extractor fans – and warn close neighbours!*

*You must have a really heavy cast-iron frying pan with a flat base – ridged ones hold the butter in the furrows, where it burns. Be brave about heating the pan over a high flame until it develops a greyish-white smoky patina before you put the fish in.*

*Wear an apron: you wouldn't catch Chef Prudhomme blackening his redfish without his kitchen whites. And tackle the dish for just two at first, at least until you know what to expect. It makes the fastest possible supper dish for a couple.*

**SERVES 2**

INGREDIENTS
*2 fillets of redfish, not less than
    2 cm/³⁄4 in thick*
*75 g/3 oz/6 tbsp butter*
*1 tsp paprika*
*½ tsp dried oregano*
*¼ tsp salt*
*good pinch each of garlic salt and cayenne*
*good grinding of black pepper*
*lime slices or lemon wedges and mixed
    salad to serve*

1 ▲ Make sure that the fillets are thoroughly thawed out if you bought them frozen. Pat them dry with kitchen paper and put them on a plate.

2 ▲ In a small pan, melt the butter and swirl in all the seasonings. Pour over the fish and turn the fish in the butter to keep it coated on both sides until you are ready to cook.

3 Put your heavy frying pan over a medium-high heat and leave it there for 5 minutes. It will smoke and develop a grey-white patina.

4 ▲ Turn the fillets once more in the butter and put them skin-side down onto the pan. Cook, pressing them down regularly with a fish slice, for 2 minutes or until the skin is crisp and very dark.

5 ▲ Pour a little of the seasoned butter over the top of each fillet and turn them over. Cook for a further 2 minutes or so, again pressing down with the fish slice.

6 Serve on hot plates, with the remaining seasoned butter poured over them, garnished with lime slices or lemon wedges and accompanied by a mixed salad.

**COOK'S TIP**

*A soft vegetable goes well with Blackened Redfish – Maque Choux or Smothered Okra, plus perhaps a Potato Salad.*

**VARIATION**

*The same method, and the same spiced butter, works well with a skinned chicken breast opened out with a series of small 'butterfly' cuts and beaten flat between 2 sheets of cling film. However, the average frying pan will take just one at a time – so when you're cooking the redfish, make a little extra of the spiced butter and keep some for a solitary supper treat on another occasion. Cook the chicken for about 3 minutes each side.*

# Fried Fish with Tartare Sauce and Hush Puppies

*The story goes that fishermen frying their catch used to drop pieces of stiffened batter into the fat to fry. They would then throw the fried batter to their dogs to hush their hungry howlings – hence the name of hush puppies, a traditional Southern food.*

**SERVES 4**

INGREDIENTS
**For the tartare sauce**
*150 ml/5 fl oz/²/₃ cup mayonnaise*
*1 tbsp chopped dill pickles*
*5 stoned green olives, chopped*
*2 spring onions, finely shredded*
*1 tbsp lemon juice*
*1–2 dashes Tabasco sauce*

**For the hush puppies**
*115 g/4 oz/1 cup cornmeal*
*50 g/2 oz/½ cup plain flour*
*1½ tsp baking powder*
*1 garlic clove, crushed with 1 tsp salt*
*2 spring onions, finely shredded*
*1 egg, lightly beaten*
*about 5 tbsp milk*
*25 g/1 oz/2 tbsp butter*

**For the fish coating**
*25 g/1 oz/¼ cup plain flour*
*25 g/1 oz/¼ cup cornflour*
*50 g/2 oz/½ cup cornmeal*
*½ tsp dried oregano*
*½ tsp dried thyme*
*1 tsp salt*
*1 tsp cayenne*
*1 tsp paprika*
*2 tsp dry mustard powder*
*1 egg*
*about 120 ml/4 fl oz/½ cup milk*

**For the fish fillets**
*oil for deep-frying*
*4 skinned plaice fillets, thawed if frozen*
*lemon slices and fresh parsley sprigs to garnish*

1 Mix all the ingredients for the tartare sauce and set aside.

2 ▲ Next make the hush puppy batter. Mix the cornmeal, flour and baking powder and stir in the crushed garlic and spring onions. Fork in the egg.

3 Heat 5 tbsp milk and the butter together slowly until the butter melts, then raise the heat and, when it boils, stir thoroughly into the dry ingredients, adding a little more milk if necessary to make a stiff dough. Leave to cool.

4 To make the fish coating, mix the flours, all the herbs and seasonings for the fish coating in a shallow dish. Beat the egg and milk together lightly in another shallow dish.

5 ▲ Scoop out pieces of hush puppy batter no bigger than a walnut and roll into balls between wetted hands.

6 ▲ Heat the oil for deep-frying. Fry the hush puppies in batches, turning them until they are deep golden brown

all over. They will swell in cooking, and it's important that they are cooked right to the middle, so don't have the oil fiercely hot to start with. It should sizzle and froth up round them as you drop them in, but not brown them immediately. Lift them out with a slotted spoon and drain on kitchen paper as they are done. Keep warm.

7 ▲ Coat the fish fillets, first in the egg mixture and then in the cornmeal mixture.

8 ▲ Fry the fillets 2 at a time for 2–3 minutes on each side, until crisp and golden brown. Drain on kitchen paper and serve with the hush puppies, garnished with lemon slices and sprigs of parsley.

**COOK'S TIP**

*Louisiana cooks use a specially fine ground cornmeal in their coating mixture. The nearest I've found to it is masa harina, from which Mexican cooks make tortillas. It's available from specialist shops or by mail order from The Cool Chile Co, Unit 7, 34 Bassett Road, London W10 6JL.*

# Salmon Courtbouillon

*This dish typifies the difference between
classical French cooking and the frugal
Creole: French cooks discard the
flavouring vegetables from the cooking
liquor, while in Louisiana all the
goodness is kept in the pot and enriched
with a dark roux that is the signature of
the local cuisine.*

*Redfish is the Creole choice for the
courtbouillon treatment because it's
firm-textured, plentiful and cheap.
Farmed salmon is equally abundant in
other areas so that's a good alternative.
Long-grain rice or pasta makes a good
accompaniment.*

**SERVES 6**

INGREDIENTS
6 salmon steaks
2 medium onions
4 celery sticks
3 bay leaves
6 sprigs fresh parsley, leaves chopped and
    stalks reserved
400 g/14 oz can tomatoes
175 ml/6 fl oz/¾ cup cooking oil
115 g/4 oz/1 cup plain flour
1 large sweet green pepper, chopped
2 garlic cloves, chopped
115 g/4 oz mushrooms, sliced
1 tsp dried thyme
1 tsp dried basil
salt and freshly ground black pepper
6 spring onions, shredded
½ lemon, thinly sliced, plus lemon wedges
    to serve

1 When you buy the salmon steaks, ask
the fishmonger for salmon trimmings
for the stock. Put these trimmings into
a deep saucepan or flameproof casserole
with 2 litres/3½ pints/9 cups cold water.

2 Peel the onions, keeping the skins.
Chop 1½ onions and put the
remaining half with the onion skins
into the pan with the salmon
trimmings. Break 1 celery stick into 3
pieces and add to the stock with 1 of the
bay leaves.

3 ▲ Bring to the boil, skimming off the
froth as it rises. When no further froth
rises, add the parsley stalks with some
salt. Simmer for 15 minutes, then
strain, discarding the solids.

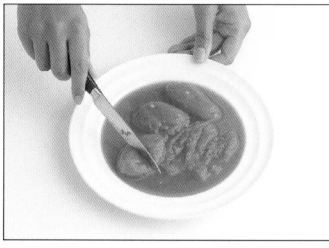

4 ▲ Thinly slice the remaining celery
sticks. Chop the canned tomatoes on a
plate, keeping all the liquor.

5 In a large saucepan or flameproof
casserole, make a roux with the oil and
flour (see Introduction). It should be a
stage darker than that in the Louisiana
Seafood Gumbo recipe.

6 ▲ The minute the roux reaches the
right stage of nutty brown, add the
chopped onions, green pepper, garlic,
remaining celery and mushrooms and
cook for a further 3 minutes.

7 ▲ Remove the roux from the heat
while you reheat the fish stock. Return
the roux to the heat and stir in the fish
stock a little at a time. Add the chopped
tomatoes, remaining 2 bay leaves, the
thyme and basil, bring to a low boil,
then simmer for 30 minutes. Check the
seasoning and correct with salt and
black pepper.

8 ▲ Put the salmon steaks into the
stock with the lemon slices and spring
onions. Cook for 5–6 minutes, until the
fish is just done. Serve hot garnished
with the chopped parsley leaves and
lemon wedges.

# Cod Steaks with Dill-Mustard Sauce

*Catfish is the favourite Deep South choice of a firm white fish. Cod is a good alternative if you are unable to buy catfish. Here it is, fried to a light golden crust in butter and served with a pungent mustard sauce.*

**SERVES 4**

INGREDIENTS
**For the sauce**
*2 tbsp Dijon mustard*
*150 ml/5 fl oz/⅔ cup mayonnaise*
*2 tbsp finely chopped fresh dill*

**For the cod steaks**
*2 tbsp milk*
*4 cod steaks*
*2 tbsp plain flour*
*2 tsp dry mustard powder*
*salt and freshly ground black pepper*
*50 g/2 oz/4 tbsp butter*
*lemon wedges and fresh dill sprigs to
    garnish*

| ▲ First mix all the ingredients for the sauce and set aside.

**2** ▲ Put the milk in a soup plate and lay the cod steaks in it. On a separate plate, mix the flour, mustard powder, salt and pepper.

**3** ▲ Melt the butter in a frying pan. Turn the cod in the milk and dip immediately in the dry coating mixture, then shake off any excess flour.

**4** ▲ When the butter sizzles, fry the cod steaks for 2–3 minutes on each side until the outside is crisp and pale golden, and you can just pull the flesh from the bone with the sharp tip of a knife.

**5** Serve straight from the pan garnished with lemon wedges and sprigs of dill. Pass the sauce at the table.

**COOK'S TIP**

*The two varieties of mustard in this recipe serve rather different functions. Mustard powder, though initially hotter, loses its heat in cooking and serves to add resonant depth of flavour and golden crispness to the coating. The Dijon in the sauce is a mellower flavour to begin with, but loses none of its flavour through cooking and contributes pungency to the sauce, which should be served at room temperature. Accompany the dish with a crisp green vegetable such as runner or French beans, or mange-tout.*

# Prawn Creole

*As sure as the Mississippi flows into the Gulf of Mexico, there'll be Prawn Creole on the Friday lunch tables of Louisiana. This is a modernized, more 'haute Creole' version based on that served at the Commander's Palace in the beautiful Garden District of New Orleans.*

**SERVES 6–8**

INGREDIENTS
75 g/3 oz/6 tbsp unsalted butter
1 large onion, halved and thinly sliced
1 large sweet green pepper, halved, seeded and thinly sliced
2 celery sticks, thinly sliced
2 garlic cloves, thinly sliced
1 bay leaf
2 tbsp paprika
450 g/1 lb/2 cups skinned, chopped fresh tomatoes
250 ml/8 fl oz/1 cup tomato juice
4 tsp Worcestershire sauce
4–6 dashes Tabasco sauce
salt
1½ tsp cornflour
1.5 kg/3 lb raw prawns, peeled and de-veined
boiled rice with optional garnish of chopped fresh parsley and shreds of lemon peel, to serve

1 ▲ Melt 25 g/1 oz/2 tbsp of the butter in a wide pan and sauté the onion, green pepper, celery, garlic and bay leaf for 1–2 minutes until all are hot and coated in butter.

2 ▲ Add the paprika, tomatoes and tomato juice, stir in the Worcestershire and Tabasco sauces, bring to the boil and simmer, uncovered, to reduce the volume by about a quarter, by which time the vegetables should have softened. Season with salt.

3 ▲ Mix the cornflour with 5 tbsp cold water in a dish and, swirling it around, pour it into the tomato sauce.

4 Stir the sauce continuously over the heat for a couple of minutes, then turn off the heat.

5 ▲ Sauté the prawns in batches in the remaining butter until pink and tender – this will take 2–4 minutes, depending on the size of the prawns.

6 ▲ Meanwhile, reheat the tomato sauce. When all the prawns are cooked, add them to the sauce and stir over the heat for no more than 1 minute. Check the seasoning and serve with fluffy boiled rice, garnished, if you like, with chopped fresh parsley and shreds of lemon peel.

**COOK'S TIP**

*Pre-cooked prawns may be all that are available, in which case incorporate all the butter into the sauce-making, skip the sauté stage and add the ready-cooked prawns to the sauce when reheating it, giving them just long enough to heat through.*

*The sauce can be made in advance to step 4 and refrigerated for reheating.*

# Oyster and Bacon Brochettes

*Six oysters per person make a good starter, served with the seasoned oyster liquor to trickle over the skewers. Increase the oyster ration to nine and serve hot with a cool salad as a lunch main course. You might then beat some olive oil into the sauce and use it to dress the salad.*

**SERVES 4–6**

INGREDIENTS
*136 oysters*
*18 thin-cut rashers rindless streaky bacon*
*115 g/4 oz/1 cup plain flour*
*1 tbsp paprika*
*1 tsp cayenne*
*1 tsp salt*
*1 tsp garlic salt*
*2 tsp dried oregano*
*freshly ground black pepper*
*oil for shallow-frying*
*celery leaves and red chillies to garnish*

**For the sauce**
*½ red chilli pepper, seeded and very finely chopped*
*2 spring onions, very finely chopped*
*2 tbsp finely chopped fresh parsley*
*liquor from shucking oysters*
*juice of ¼–½ lemon*
*salt and freshly ground black pepper*

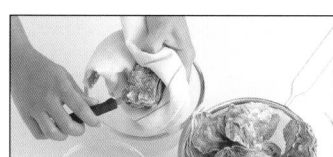

1 ▲ Shuck the oysters over a bowl to catch their liquor for the sauce. Wrap your left hand in a clean tea towel and cup the deep shell of each oyster in your wrapped hand. Work the point of a strong short-bladed knife into the hinge between the shells and twist.

2 ▲ Push the knife in and work it to cut the muscle, holding the shell closed. Tip the liquor from the deep shell into the bowl.

3 ▲ Cut under the flesh of the oyster to free it from the shell. Discard the drained shells.

4 ▲ Halve the bacon rashers across and wrap each oyster in half a rasher, then thread them onto 4 or 6 skewers.

5 ▲ Make the sauce next. Mix the chopped chilli, spring onions and parsley into the bowl of oyster liquor and sharpen to taste with lemon juice. Season and transfer to a small bowl.

6 ▲ Mix the flour with the paprika, cayenne, salt, garlic salt, oregano and a good grinding of black pepper. Spread on a flat plate and roll the skewered oysters in it, shaking the surplus back onto the plate.

7 Heat 2.5 cm/1 in depth of oil in a wide frying pan and fry the skewers, in batches if necessary, over a medium-high heat, turning until they are crisp and brown all round. They should take 3–4 minutes each.

8 Drain the skewers on kitchen paper and serve with the garnish and accompanied by the little bowl of sauce.

**COOK'S TIP**

*Individual oysters can be skewered and cooked on cocktail sticks to serve hot as the smartest of canapés. Pass the sauce with them in a little bowl for dipping.*

# Mussel and Artichoke Casserole

*New Orleans cooks use oysters and their liquor, but plump golden mussels deliver a sea-scented liquor that is just as delicious with sweet-flavoured artichoke hearts, particularly when cooked in white wine.*

*Serve with plenty of hot French bread as a satisfying one-pot meal, followed by a salad.*

**SERVES 4**

INGREDIENTS
*2 kg/4½ lb mussels*
*6–8 sprigs fresh parsley*
*2 bay leaves*
*120 ml/4 fl oz/½ cup white wine*
*400 g/14 oz can artichoke hearts*
*50 g/2 oz/4 tbsp butter*
*50 g/2 oz/½ cup plain flour*
*salt and freshly ground black pepper*
*6 spring onions, roughly chopped*
*3 tbsp fresh white breadcrumbs*
*3 tbsp grated Parmesan cheese*

1  Clean the mussels (see Louisiana Seafood Gumbo for the method).

2  ▲ Cut the leaves from the parsley, keeping the stalks. Chop the leaves roughly and set aside. Put the stalks into a deep saucepan with the bay leaves and wine. Drain the artichoke hearts and set aside, keeping their liquor. Add 120 ml/4 fl oz/½ cup of the liquor to the pot and bring to the boil.

3  ▲ Cook the mussels in batches in the pot over a high heat, shaking the covered pot (see Louisiana Seafood Gumbo, for the method). Use tongs to lift the mussels as they open into a large sieve set over a bowl.

4  ▲ Shell the mussels, keeping any liquor that drips through into the bowl.

5  When all the mussels are shelled, pour the liquor from the pot through the sieve, discarding the solids.

6  ▲ Quarter the artichoke hearts.

7  Reheat the strained mussel liquor. Meanwhile, preheat the grill and set the grill shelf low.

8  ▲ In a heavy pan, make a roux with the butter and flour (see Introduction). As soon as it is pale golden, remove the pan from the heat and slowly begin adding the mussel liquor, a little at a time, stirring constantly.

9  Return to a gentle heat when the sauce loosens and smooths out and continue to stir in liquor a little at a time. Simmer to a creamy sauce. Check the seasoning.

10  Stir the mussels, artichoke hearts, spring onions and most of the chopped parsley leaves gently into the sauce and pour into a flameproof dish.

11  Mix the breadcrumbs and Parmesan and sprinkle evenly over the dish. Grill, watching constantly, until the top is golden. Garnish with the remaining chopped parsley leaves and serve immediately from the dish.

# Trout Meunière with Pecan Butter

*The Louisiana version of the French
trout with almonds.*

**SERVES 4**

INGREDIENTS
**For the pecan butter**
*50 g/2 oz/½ cup shelled pecan halves*
*50 g/2 oz/4 tbsp unsalted butter*
*2 tsp Worcestershire sauce*
*1 tsp lemon juice*

**For the trout fillets**
*4 large fillets of trout*
*2 tsp paprika*
*1 tsp cayenne*
*1 tsp dried oregano*
*pinch of dried thyme*
*½ tsp garlic salt*
*1 tsp salt*
*freshly ground black pepper*
*1 egg*
*120 ml/4 fl oz/½ cup milk*
*3 tbsp plain flour*
*oil for shallow-frying*

1 ▲ Make the pecan butter first.
Preheat the oven to 180°C/350°F/Gas 4.
Spread the pecans on a baking sheet
and roast in the oven for 15–20
minutes. Set aside to cool.

2 Whizz the roasted pecans in bursts in
a food processor or blender to chop
quite finely. Add the butter,
Worcestershire sauce and lemon juice
and blend thoroughly.

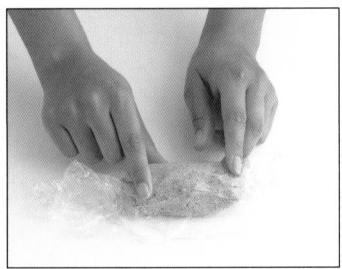

3 ▲ Scrape out the pecan butter onto
cling film, roll into a column, wrap and
chill until required.

4 Rinse the trout fillets under the cold
tap, then dry. Remove any remaining
bones.

5 In a cup or small bowl, mix the
paprika, cayenne, oregano, thyme,
garlic salt, salt and a good grinding of
black pepper. Sprinkle a pinch or two
over each fillet.

6 ▲ Lightly beat the egg and milk
together in a shallow dish and beat in
1 tsp of the seasoning mix.

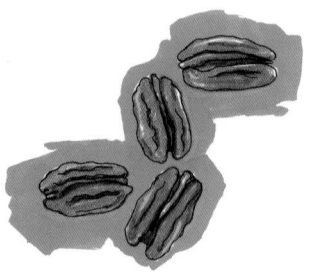

7 ▲ In another shallow dish, combine
the remaining seasoning mix
thoroughly with the flour.

8 Heat the oil for shallow-frying in a
frying pan.

9 ▲ Pass the trout fillets through the
egg-wash mixture, then through the
seasoned flour, shaking off any excess.
Fry them, then drain them on kitchen
paper and keep them warm.

10 ▲ Unwrap the chilled butter and cut
into coin-thick slices.

11 Serve the fillets with a slice of pecan
butter on top of each one.

# Meat, Poultry & Game

*Game was of primary importance to the early settlers in Louisiana, both for Cajuns, who hunted for their own food, and Creoles, who had it caught and cooked for their tables. Now, on a day-to-day basis domesticated chicken, duck and poussin and farmed quail replace the feathered wild game that once formed the main source of meat. Louisianans are keen, too, on pork: the pig was introduced to America by the first settlers from Europe.*

# Chicken and Prawn Jambalaya

*The mixture of chicken, seafood and rice suggests a close relationship to the Spanish paella, but the name is more probably derived from 'jambon' (the French for ham), 'à la ya' (Creole for rice). Jambalayas are a colourful mixture of highly flavoured ingredients, and are always made in large quantities for big family or celebration meals.*

**SERVES 10**

INGREDIENTS

*2 × 1.5 kg/3 lb chicken*
*salt and freshly ground black pepper*
*450 g/1 lb piece raw smoked gammon*
*50 g/2 oz/4 tbsp lard or bacon fat*
*50 g/2 oz/½ cup plain flour*
*3 medium onions, finely sliced*
*2 sweet green peppers, seeded and sliced*
*675 g/1½ lb tomatoes, skinned and chopped*
*2–3 garlic cloves, crushed*
*2 tsp chopped fresh thyme or 1 tsp dried thyme*
*24 Mediterranean prawns, beheaded and peeled*
*500 g/1¼ lb/3 cups American long-grain rice*
*2–3 dashes Tabasco sauce*
*1 bunch spring onions, finely chopped (including the green parts)*
*3 tbsp chopped fresh parsley*

1 ▲ Cut each chicken into 10 pieces and season with salt and pepper.

2 ▲ Dice the gammon, discarding the rind and fat.

3 ▲ In a large heavy-based pan or flameproof casserole, melt the lard or bacon fat and brown the chicken pieces all over, lifting them out with a slotted spoon and setting them aside as they are done.

4 ▲ Turn the heat down, sprinkle the flour onto the fat in the pan and stir continuously until the roux turns light golden brown (see Introduction).

5 ▲ Return the chicken pieces to the pan, add the diced gammon, onions, green peppers, tomatoes, garlic and thyme and cook, stirring regularly, for 10 minutes, then stir in the prawns.

6 Stir the rice into the pan with one and a half times the rice's volume in cold water. Season with salt, pepper and Tabasco sauce. Bring to the boil and cook over a gentle heat until the rice is tender and the liquid absorbed. Add a little extra boiling water if the rice looks like drying out before it is cooked.

7 Mix the spring onions and parsley into the finished dish, reserving a little of the mixture to scatter over the jambalaya. Serve hot.

**COOK'S TIP**

*The roux thickening is a vital part of Cajun cooking, particularly essential to jambalaya. Cook the roux over a low heat, watching like a hawk to see it doesn't develop dark flecks, which indicate burning. Don't stop stirring for an instant.*

# Duck Breasts with Red Pepper Jelly Glaze
# and Grilled Sweet Potatoes

*Sweet potatoes have pinkish skins and flesh varying from creamy white to deep orange. Choose a long cylindrically-shaped tuber for the neatest disks.*

**SERVES 2**

INGREDIENTS
*2 duck breast fillets*
*coarse sea salt and freshly ground black*
*    pepper*
*1 pink-skinned sweet potato weighing*
*    about 400 g/14 oz*
*2 tbsp Red Pepper Jelly (see Snacks,*
*    Starters and Sauces, for the recipe)*
*1 tbsp sherry vinegar*
*50 g/2 oz/4 tbsp butter, melted*
*    green salad to serve*

I ▲ Slash the skin of the duck breasts diagonally at 2.5 cm/1 in intervals and rub salt and pepper over the skin and into the cuts.

2 Preheat the grill with the shelf set so that the meat will be 7.5–10 cm/ 3–4 in from the heat.

3 ▲ Scrub the sweet potato and cut into 1 cm/½ in thick slices, discarding the rounded ends.

4 Grill the meat, skin-side up first, for 5 minutes, then flesh-side up for 8–10 minutes, according to how pink you like your duck.

5 ▲ Meanwhile, warm the jelly and vinegar together in a bowl set in a pan of hot water, stirring to mix them as the jelly melts.

**COOK'S TIP**

*Pork chops are also good grilled and caramelized with the jelly, and the grilled sweet potatoes are excellent with them. Sweet potatoes also go well with grilled gammon rashers for a quick supper.*

6 ▲ Remove the grill pan from the heat, turn the duck breasts skin-side up and paint with the jelly mixture. Return to the grill and cook for a further 2–3 minutes until the glaze caramelizes. Transfer the duck breasts to a serving plate and keep warm.

7 ▲ Brush the sweet potato slices with melted butter and arrange in the grill pan. Sprinkle with coarse sea salt and place one level higher under the grill than the duck breasts were.

8 Cook the sweet potatoes for 4–5 minutes on each side until soft, brushing with more butter and sprinkling with sea salt and black pepper when you turn them.

9 Serve the duck breasts sliced with the sweet potatoes and a green salad.

# Smothered Rabbit

*Game has always formed a big part of the Cajun diet – it was the only meat available to the early settlers. The smothering technique gives plenty of flavour to a domestic rabbit, too. Get your butcher or game dealer to prepare the rabbit pieces for you.*

**SERVES 4**

INGREDIENTS

*1 rabbit, skinned, cleaned and cut into 8 pieces*
*2 tsp salt*
*½ tsp garlic salt*
*½ tsp dried oregano*
*good pinch each of freshly ground black pepper and cayenne*
*50 g/2 oz/½ cup plain flour*
*4 tbsp cooking oil*
*1 medium onion, chopped*
*1 celery stick, chopped*
*1 large garlic clove, crushed*
*1 bay leaf*
*350 ml/12 fl oz/1½ cups chicken stock*
*3 spring onions, shredded*
*2 tbsp chopped fresh parsley*
*mange-tout to serve*

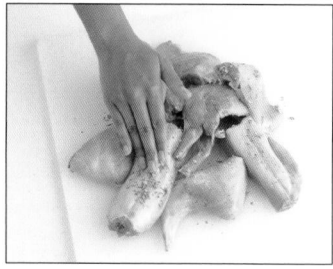

1 ▲ Mix the salt, garlic salt, oregano, black pepper and cayenne together. Sprinkle the rabbit pieces lightly, using about half the seasoning mix, and pat it in with your fingers.

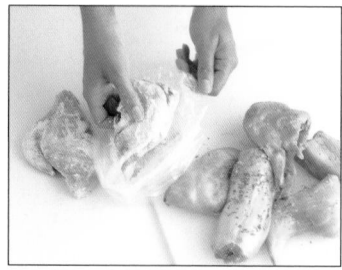

2 ▲ Put the rest of the seasoning mix with the flour into a polythene bag, shake to mix, then shake the pieces of rabbit in this to dredge them, shaking the surplus back into the bag as you lift them out.

3 ▲ Heat the oil in a heavy flameproof casserole and fry the rabbit pieces until browned on all sides. Do this in batches so as not to crowd the pan, removing each one as it is ready.

4 ▲ When all the rabbit is browned, cook the onion and celery in the same pan for 5 minutes, stirring regularly. Add the garlic and bay leaf.

5 Heat the stock. Meanwhile, add 1 tbsp seasoned flour to the oil in the pan and stir over the heat for 1 minute. Remove from the heat and gradually stir in some of the hot stock. When the sauce loosens, return the pan to the heat and add the remaining stock, stirring constantly until boiling point is reached.

6 Lower the heat, return the rabbit pieces to the casserole, cover and simmer for about 1 hour, until the rabbit is very tender.

7 ▲ Check the seasoning and stir in the spring onions and parsley. Serve with mange-tout and perhaps some crusty bread.

**COOK'S TIP**

*You could make Smothered Chicken in exactly the same way with 4 chicken pieces.*

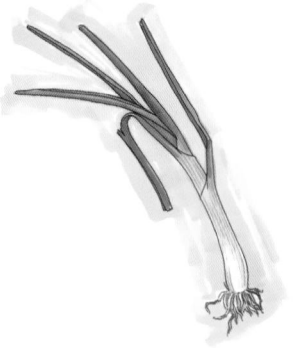

# Chicken Sauce Piquante

*Sauce Piquante goes with everything that runs, flies or swims in Louisiana – you will even find Alligator Sauce Piquante on menus. It is based on the brown Cajun roux and has chilli peppers to give it heat: vary the heat by the number you use.*

**SERVES 4**

INGREDIENTS
*4 chicken legs or 2 legs and 2 breasts*
*5 tbsp cooking oil*
*50 g/2 oz/½ cup plain flour*
*1 medium onion, chopped*
*2 celery sticks, sliced*
*1 sweet green pepper, seeded and diced*
*2 garlic cloves, crushed*
*1 bay leaf*
*½ tsp dried thyme*
*½ tsp dried oregano*
*1–2 red chilli peppers, seeded and finely chopped*
*400 g/14 oz can tomatoes, chopped, with their juice*
*300 ml/10 fl oz/1¼ cups chicken stock*
*salt and freshly ground black pepper*
*watercress to garnish*
*boiled potatoes to serve*

**1** ▲ Halve the chicken legs through the joint, or the breasts across the middle, to give 8 pieces.

**2** ▲ In a heavy frying pan, fry the chicken pieces in the oil until brown on all sides, lifting them out and setting them aside as they are done.

**3** Strain the oil from the pan into a heavy flameproof casserole. Heat it and stir in the flour. Stir constantly over a low heat until the roux is the colour of peanut butter (see Introduction).

**4** ▲ Immediately the roux reaches the right stage, tip in the onion, celery and sweet pepper and stir over the heat for 2–3 minutes.

**5** ▲ Add the garlic, bay leaf, thyme, oregano and chilli pepper(s). Stir for 1 minute, then turn down the heat and stir in the tomatoes with their juice.

**6** Return the casserole to the heat and gradually stir in the stock. Add the chicken pieces, cover and leave to simmer for 45 minutes, until the chicken is tender.

**7** If there is too much sauce or it is too runny, remove the lid for the last 10–15 minutes of the cooking time and raise the heat a little.

**8** Check the seasoning and serve garnished with watercress and accompanied by boiled potatoes, or perhaps rice or pasta, and a green vegetable or salad of your choice.

**COOK'S TIP**

*If you prefer to err on the side of caution with chilli heat, use just 1 chilli pepper and hot up the seasoning at the end with a dash or two of Tabasco sauce.*
    *The oil in chilli peppers clings to your skin and could hurt if you then rub your eyes. Always scrape out the seeds under running cold water and wash your hands after handling chillies.*

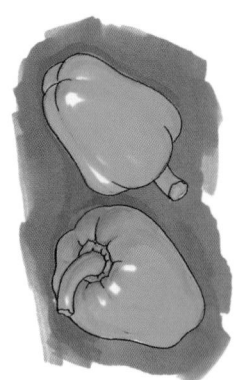

# Poussins with Dirty Rice

*This rice is called dirty not because of the bits in it (though the roux and chicken livers do 'muss' it up a bit) but because jazz is called 'dirty music', and the rice here is certainly jazzed up.*

**SERVES 4**

INGREDIENTS
**For the rice**
*4 tbsp cooking oil*
*25 g/1 oz/¼ cup plain flour*
*50 g/2 oz/4 tbsp butter*
*1 large onion, chopped*
*2 celery sticks, chopped*
*1 sweet green pepper, seeded and diced*
*2 garlic cloves, crushed*
*200 g/7 oz minced pork*
*225 g/8 oz chicken livers, trimmed and sliced*
*salt, freshly ground black pepper and Tabasco sauce*
*300 ml/10 fl oz/1¼ cups chicken stock*
*4 spring onions, shredded*
*3 tbsp chopped fresh parsley*
*225 g/8 oz/generous 1 cup American long-grain rice, cooked*

**For the birds**
*4 poussins*
*2 bay leaves, halved*
*25 g/1 oz/2 tbsp butter*
*salt and freshly ground black pepper*
*1 lemon*

1 In a small heavy saucepan, make a roux with 2 tbsp of the oil and the flour (see Introduction). When it is a chestnut-brown colour, remove the pan from the heat and place it immediately on a cold surface.

2 ▲ Heat the remaining 2 tbsp oil with the butter in a frying pan and stir-fry the onion, celery and sweet pepper for about 5 minutes.

3 Add the garlic and pork and stir-fry for 5 minutes, breaking up the pork and stirring to cook it all over.

4 ▲ Add the chicken livers and fry for 2–3 minutes until they have changed colour all over. Season with salt, pepper and a dash of Tabasco sauce.

5 ▲ Stir the roux into the stir-fried mixture, then gradually add in the stock. When it begins to bubble, cover and cook for 30 minutes, stirring occasionally. Then uncover and cook for a further 15 minutes, stirring frequently.

6 Preheat the oven to 200°C/400°F/Gas 6. Mix the spring onions and parsley into the meat mixture and stir it all into the cooked rice.

7 ▲ Put ½ bay leaf and 1 tbsp rice into each poussin. Rub the outside with the butter and season with salt and pepper.

8 ▲ Put the birds on a rack in a roasting tin, squeeze the juice from the lemon over them and roast in the oven for 35–40 minutes, basting twice with the pan juices.

9 Put the remaining rice into a shallow ovenproof dish, cover it and place on a low shelf in the oven for the last 15–20 minutes of the birds' cooking time.

10 Serve the birds on a bed of dirty rice with the roasting pan juices (drained of fat) poured over.

**COOK'S TIP**

*You can substitute quails for the poussins, in which case offer 2 per person and stuff each little bird with 2 tsp of the dirty rice before roasting for about 20 minutes.*

# Pork Chops with Lemon and Garlic Grilling Sauce

*Another recipe from the McIlhenny family, producers of Tabasco sauce. They like their food on the hot side: cautious cooks can start off with less Tabasco in the mixture, adding a dash or two more at the end to get it right.*

**SERVES 4**

INGREDIENTS
*4 pork chops*
*115 g/4 oz/½ cup butter*
*½ lemon*
*1 tbsp Worcestershire sauce*
*1½ tsp Tabasco sauce*
*1 garlic clove, finely chopped*
*salt and freshly ground black pepper*
*grilled sweet peppers and tomatoes to serve*

I  Preheat the grill. Arrange the chops in the grill pan, but do not place them under the grill.

2 ▲ Melt the butter in a small non-aluminium saucepan. Squeeze in the juice of the lemon and bring to simmering point.

3 ▲ Add the Worcestershire and Tabasco sauces and the garlic and continue cooking over a low heat, without browning the garlic, for 5 minutes or so. Season with salt and pepper.

4 ▲ Brush the tops of the chops liberally with the sauce, place the pan under the grill and grill until they begin to brown – about 5 minutes.

5 ▲ Turn the chops and brush with more sauce. Grill for a further 5 minutes or so, depending on the thickness of the chops. You can trickle a little more of the sauce over to serve. Accompany the chops with grilled sweet peppers and tomatoes.

**COOK'S TIP**

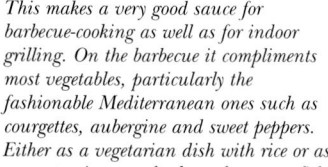

*This makes a very good sauce for barbecue-cooking as well as for indoor grilling. On the barbecue it compliments most vegetables, particularly the fashionable Mediterranean ones such as courgettes, aubergine and sweet peppers. Either as a vegetarian dish with rice or as accompaniment to barbecued meat or fish, you could assemble such vegetables in chunks on skewers and baste with the sauce while turning over the coals.*

*Under the grill, the sauce is just as good with chicken pieces, duck breasts or lamb steaks as it is with pork.*

# Roast Pork with Cajun Stuffing

*The familiar trinity of onion, celery and sweet green pepper gives Cajun flavour to a handsome roast complete with crackling.*

**SERVES 6**

INGREDIENTS
*1.5 kg/3½ lb boned loin of pork*
*1 tbsp salt*
*1 tsp each freshly ground black pepper,*
   *cayenne, paprika and dried oregano*
*2 tbsp cooking oil or 25 g/1 oz/2 tbsp lard*
*1 small onion, finely chopped*
*1 celery stick, finely chopped*
*½ sweet green pepper, seeded and finely*
   *chopped*
*1 garlic clove, crushed*

**I ▲** If the pork is already tied up, then untie it. Score the pork skin closely to make good crackling (you can ask your butcher to do this). Rub 2 tsp of the salt into the skin the night before if you can; or, if not, as far in advance of cooking as possible on the day. If the meat has been refrigerated overnight, let it stand in an airy place at room temperature for a couple of hours or so before cooking.

**2 ▲** Preheat the oven to 220°C/425°F/Gas 7. Mix the black pepper, cayenne, paprika and oregano with the remaining 1 tsp salt and rub over the meaty side of the meat.

**3** Heat the oil or lard and gently fry the onion, celery and sweet pepper for 5 minutes, adding the garlic for the last minute.

**4 ▲** Spread the vegetables over the inside of the meat.

**5 ▲** Roll up the meat skin-side out and tie in several places.

**6** Roast the meat on a rack in a roasting tin. After 30 minutes reduce the heat to 180°C/350°F/Gas 4. Baste with the pan juices after 15 minutes and again every 20 minutes or so.

**7 ▲** The overall roasting time is about 2 hours. If the crackling doesn't go crisp and bubbly in the latter stages, raise the oven heat a little for the last 20–30 minutes.

**8** Allow the meat to rest in a warm place for 10–15 minutes before carving.

**COOK'S TIP**

*You can roast potatoes or sweet potatoes in the tin with the meat, or bake them in their skins alongside the meat in the oven. Skim some of the fat from the pan juice and bubble what's left with some red wine and a bay leaf to make a tasty gravy.*

# Pan-fried Veal with Fettuccine

*An old Creole dish with obvious European antecedents.*

## SERVES 4

INGREDIENTS
*4 thin-cut escalopes of veal, each weighing about 100 g/3½ oz*
*salt, freshly ground black pepper and cayenne*
*2 eggs*
*120 ml/l4 fl oz/½ cup milk*
*2 tbsp finely grated Parmesan cheese*
*50 g/2 oz/½ cup plain flour*
*115 g/4 oz/1 cup breadcrumbs*
*50 g/2 oz/4 tbsp butter*
*2 tbsp cooking oil*
*green salad to serve*

**For the fettucine**
*salt*
*225 g/8 oz dried or 350 g/12 oz fresh fettucine*
*50 g/2 oz/4 tbsp butter*
*3 tbsp finely chopped fresh parsley (optional)*
*freshly ground black pepper and cayenne*

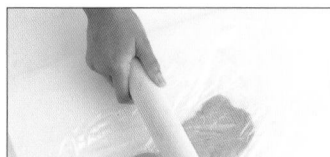

I ▲ Sandwich each veal escalope between 2 sheets of cling film and beat out flat with a rolling pin or the flat side of a meat cleaver. Season the veal with salt, black pepper and cayenne.

2 Beat the eggs lightly with the milk and grated Parmesan in a shallow dish. Spread the flour and the breadcrumbs on separate plates.

3 Bring a large pan of salted water to the boil for the pasta. Meanwhile, melt half the butter in half the oil in a heavy frying pan.

4 ▲ You will have to cook the veal escalopes one at a time, so prepare each one as you go. Dredge it lightly with flour by turning it in the plate of flour and shaking off the excess.

5 ▲ Pass the escalope through the eggwash, allowing the excess to drip briefly back into the dish.

6 ▲ Turn the escalope in the bread-crumbs, then drop immediately into the frying pan and cook for 2 minutes on each side. Drain on kitchen paper and keep warm. Cook the remaining esca-lopes in the same way, adding more butter and oil to the pan as necessary.

7 ▲ Meanwhile cook the fettuccine: fresh pasta will take only 2–3 minutes, dried pasta up to 10 minutes.

8 When the pasta is *al dente* (that is, tender but still having some firmness of bite), drain thoroughly, return to the pan and drop in the butter.

9 When the butter melts, toss this and the parsley (if you are using it) through the pasta and spoon into a warm serving bowl. Add a little black pepper and a sprinkling of cayenne.

10 Serve the veal with the fettuccine and a green salad.

## COOK'S TIP

*The escalopes could be cut from a turkey breast if you prefer.*

# Vegetables

Cajuns love all the sweet-tasting vegetables – corn, sweet potatoes, sweet root vegetables, such as parsnips, and, of course, sweet peppers. Sweet green pepper, celery and onion are affectionately called the 'Holy Trinity', and together they form the cornerstone of Cajun culinary tradition. Some vegetables are particularly valued for their soft, melting texture. This fondness for succulence can lead to what, to outsiders, seems an over-cooking of vegetables, and I have modified this where I believe that modern tastes prefer an element of crispness, particularly in green vegetables such as cabbage. Salads are also a big feature of the Louisiana table, usually large, hearty and hotly spiced with mustard and cayenne or Tabasco sauce.

# Vinegared Chilli Cabbage

**SERVES 4–6**

INGREDIENTS
*1 fresh red chilli pepper, halved, seeded
and shredded
25 g/1 oz/2 tbsp lard or butter
2 garlic cloves, crushed (optional)
1 medium white cabbage, cored and
shredded
salt
2 tsp cider vinegar
1 tsp cayenne*

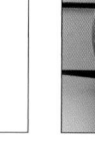

1 ▲ Put the chilli with the lard or butter into a large pan and cook over medium heat until the chilli sizzles and curls at the edges.

**COOK'S TIP**

*A wok with a domed lid is good for this part-frying, part-steaming method of cooking cabbage.*

2 ▲ Add the garlic and cabbage and stir, over the heat, until the cabbage is thoroughly coated and warm. Add salt to taste and 5 tbsp water. Bring to the boil, cover and lower the heat.

3 Cook, shaking the pan regularly, for 3–4 minutes until the cabbage wilts. Remove the lid, raise the heat and cook off the liquid. Check the seasoning and add more salt if necessary. Sprinkle with vinegar and cayenne.

# Coleslaw in Triple-Hot Dressing

*The triple hotness is supplied by mustard, horseradish and Tabasco.*

**SERVES 6**

INGREDIENTS
*½ white cabbage, cored and shredded
2 celery sticks, finely sliced
1 sweet green pepper, seeded and finely
sliced
4 spring onions, shredded
2 tbsp chopped fresh dill
cayenne*

**For the dressing**
*1 tbsp Dijon mustard
2 tsp creamed horseradish
1 tsp Tabasco sauce
2 tbsp red wine vinegar
5 tbsp olive oil
salt and freshly ground black pepper*

1 Mix the cabbage, celery, green pepper and spring onions in a large salad bowl.

2 ▲ Make the dressing. In a small bowl, mix the mustard, horseradish and Tabasco sauce, then gradually stir in the vinegar with a fork and finally beat in the olive oil and seasoning. Toss the salad in the dressing and leave to stand, if possible, for at least an hour. During this time turn the salad once or twice in its dressing.

3 Immediately before serving, season the salad if necessary, toss again and sprinkle with dill and cayenne.

**COOK'S TIP**

*This is a good salad for a buffet table or picnic as it improves with some standing in its dressing (could be overnight in the fridge) and travels well in a covered plastic bowl or box.*

*Vinegared Chilli Cabbage (top) and Coleslaw in Triple-Hot Dressing (bottom).*

# Potato Salad

*Served in Cajun country not just with cold meats or grills, but as an essential side dish to a bowl of gumbo.*

**SERVES 6–8**

INGREDIENTS
*8 medium waxy potatoes*
*1 sweet green pepper, seeded and diced*
*1 large pickled gherkin, chopped*
*4 spring onions, shredded*
*3 hard-boiled eggs, shelled and chopped*
*250 ml/8 fl oz/1 cup mayonnaise*
*1 tbsp Dijon mustard*
*salt and freshly ground black pepper*
*Tabasco sauce*
*cayenne*

1  Wash the potatoes and cook them in their skins in salted water. Drain when tender, and when they are cool enough skin them and dice coarsely.

2  ▲  Mix the potatoes in a salad bowl with the green pepper, gherkin, spring onions and hard-boiled eggs.

3  ▲  In a separate bowl, mix the mayonnaise with the mustard and season with salt, black pepper and Tabasco sauce to taste.

4  Toss the dressing gently through the salad and sprinkle the top with a pinch or two of cayenne.

# Smothered Okra

**SERVES 4–6**

INGREDIENTS
*500 g/1¼ lb okra*
*1 red onion, thinly sliced*
*25 g/1 oz/2 tbsp butter*
*1 garlic clove, crushed*
*4 large tomatoes, skinned, seeded and chopped*
*1 tsp red wine vinegar*
*salt*
*freshly ground black pepper and cayenne*

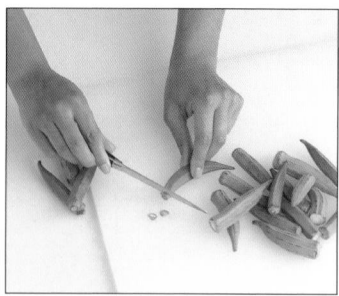

1  ▲  Trim the okra, cutting the stem end of each one just level with the pod.

2  Soften the onion in the butter, stirring regularly over a low heat for 5–10 minutes. Add the garlic, stir for a further minute, then add the tomatoes, vinegar, 120 ml/4 fl oz/½ cup water and salt, and stew, uncovered, until it becomes a thick sauce.

3  ▲  Stir in the okra, cover and cook over a very low heat for about 25 minutes, checking half-way through and adding a little more water if it is drying out – the sauce should be rather thick. When the okra are quite soft, season to taste with black pepper and cayenne. Serve hot.

*Potato Salad (top) and Smothered Okra (bottom).*

# Maque Choux

*A Cajun classic, good with ham and chicken. Some cooks add a little sugar to heighten the sweetness, but for most the natural sweetness of the corn is enough.*

**SERVES 4–6**

INGREDIENTS
*50 g/2 oz/4 tbsp butter*
*1 large onion, finely chopped*
*1 sweet green pepper, seeded and diced*
*2 large tomatoes, skinned and chopped*
*450 g/1 lb/4 cups frozen sweetcorn*
  *kernels, thawed*
*120 ml/4 fl oz/½ cup milk*
*salt, freshly ground black pepper and*
  *cayenne*

1 ▲ Melt half the butter in a large pan and soften the onion in it, stirring regularly over a low heat for about 10 minutes until it begins to turn pale gold. Add the sweet pepper and stir over the heat for a further minute, then add the tomatoes and leave to cook gently while you prepare the corn.

2 ▲ Put the corn kernels and milk into a food processor or blender and process in brief bursts to break up the kernels to a porridgy consistency.

3 ▲ Stir the corn mixture thoroughly into the pan and cook, partially covered, over a low heat for 20 minutes. Stir regularly, making sure that it does not stick to the bottom. If the mixture threatens to become too dry, add a little more milk. Should it still be rather wet in the latter stages, uncover, raise the heat a little and stir constantly for the last 5 minutes.

4 Stir in the rest of the butter and season quite highly with salt, black pepper and cayenne. Serve hot.

**COOK'S TIP**

*You are aiming at a consistency rather like that of scrambled eggs and, like scrambled eggs, Maque Choux is also good with bacon and fried bread for breakfast.*

# Potatoes, Peppers and Shallots Roasted with Rosemary

*Based on a dish which is served at the Commander's Palace, this is in the new, rather more elegant style of New Orleans restaurant cooking.*

**SERVES 4**

INGREDIENTS
*500 g/1¼ lb waxy potatoes*
*12 shallots*
*2 sweet yellow peppers*
*corn oil or olive oil*
*2 sprigs fresh rosemary*
*salt and freshly ground black pepper*

1 Preheat the oven to 200°C/400°F/ Gas 6. Wash the potatoes and blanch for 5 minutes in boiling water. Drain and, when they are cool enough to handle, skin them and halve lengthways.

2 ▲ Peel the shallots, allowing them to fall into their natural segments. Cut each sweet pepper lengthways into 8 strips, discarding the seeds and pith.

**COOK'S TIP**

*They don't eat much lamb in Louisiana, but if they did this would certainly be a fine all-in-one vegetable dish to accompany it. It's also good with roast chicken.*

3 ▲ Oil a shallow ovenproof dish thoroughly with corn or olive oil (corn is more authentic, olive tastes better). Assemble the potatoes and peppers in alternating rows and stud with the shallots.

4 ▲ Cut the rosemary sprigs into 5 cm/ 2 in lengths and tuck among the vegetables. Season the dish generously with olive oil, salt and pepper and bake in the oven, uncovered, for 30–40 minutes until all the vegetables are tender.

# Red Beans and Rice

*This is the classic Monday dish in Louisiana; Monday being washday and beans not minding being left to their own devices for as long as it takes to finish the laundry. Hardly worth making in small quantities because of the long cooking time, this makes a splendid supper-party dish served with good grilled sausages and a green salad.*

**SERVES 8–10**

INGREDIENTS
*500 g/1¼ lb/3⅓ cups dried red kidney
  beans*
*2 bay leaves*
*2 tbsp oil, bacon fat or lard*
*1 medium onion, chopped*
*2 garlic cloves, finely chopped*
*2 celery sticks, sliced*
*225 g/8 oz piece salt pork or raw ham*
*salt and freshly ground black pepper*
*450 g/1 lb/2¼ cups American long-
  grain rice*
*3 tbsp chopped fresh parsley*

I ▲ Start the night before. Wash the beans thoroughly in a colander under a running cold tap, then put them into a deep bowl and fill it to the top with cold water. Leave to stand overnight.

2 Drain the beans and put them into a large pan with fresh cold water to cover generously. Bring to the boil and boil hard for 10 minutes, then drain and rinse both the beans and the pan.

3 Return the beans to the pan with the bay leaves and fresh cold water to cover generously. Bring to the boil, reduce the heat and simmer for 30 minutes, uncovered, topping up the water if necessary.

4 Meanwhile heat the oil or fat in a frying pan and cook the onion, garlic and celery gently, stirring frequently, until the onion is soft and translucent.

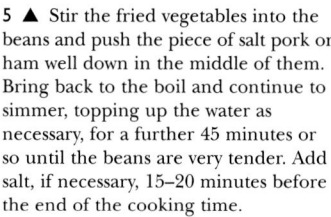

5 ▲ Stir the fried vegetables into the beans and push the piece of salt pork or ham well down in the middle of them. Bring back to the boil and continue to simmer, topping up the water as necessary, for a further 45 minutes or so until the beans are very tender. Add salt, if necessary, 15–20 minutes before the end of the cooking time.

6 Measure the rice into a pan with a cup and add 1½ times its volume of cold water, plus 1 tsp salt. Bring to the boil, stirring occasionally, then cover the pan tightly and leave over a very low heat for 12 minutes. Without lifting the lid, turn off the heat and leave the rice undisturbed for a further 12 minutes.

7 ▲ Lift the piece of salt pork or ham out from among the beans and dice it, removing the fat and rind. Drain the beans and correct the seasoning with plenty of black pepper and more salt if necessary. Mix the diced meat through the beans.

8 ▲ Fork up the rice to make it fluffy, stir in the parsley, then mound it in a warm serving dish and pour the beans over the top.

**COOK'S TIP**

*The first fast boiling is a safety measure to eliminate toxins present in red kidney beans, so don't skip it.*

*The beans are just as good made the day before and reheated when you cook the rice. Indeed, some Cajun cooks say that this makes them taste even better.*

# Spiced Aubergine Fried in Cornmeal

**SERVES 3–4**

INGREDIENTS

*1 large aubergine*
*salt*
*1 egg*
*120 ml/4 fl oz/½ cup milk*
*½ tsp paprika*
*½ tsp cayenne*
*½ tsp freshly ground black pepper*
*½ tsp garlic salt*
*115 g/4 oz/1 cup fine cornmeal*
*oil for deep-frying*

1 ▲ Cut the aubergine into 1 cm/½ in thick slices. Sprinkle lightly with salt and stack them in a colander. Leave standing in the sink to drain for 30 minutes, then wipe the slices dry on kitchen paper.

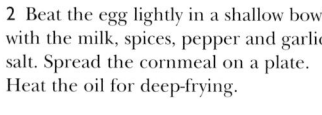

2 Beat the egg lightly in a shallow bowl with the milk, spices, pepper and garlic salt. Spread the cornmeal on a plate. Heat the oil for deep-frying.

3 ▲ Pass each slice of aubergine through the spiced egg mixture, allowing the excess briefly to drip back into the bowl. Turn the slice in the cornmeal, then drop immediately into the hot oil.

4 ▲ Fry 3 or 4 slices at a time, turning once, until they are golden on both sides. Drain thoroughly on kitchen paper and keep warm until all the slices are fried. Serve hot.

**COOK'S TIP**

*The crisp aubergine slices are very good with plain grills of meat, poultry or fish. They can also substitute for meat in a vegetarian meal.*

# Baked Sweet Potatoes

*Sweet potatoes go well with the favourite Cajun seasonings: plenty of salt, white pepper as well as black and cayenne, and lavish quantities of butter. Serve half a potato per person as an accompaniment to meat, sausages or fish, or a whole one as a supper dish, perhaps topped with crisped and crumbled bacon and accompanied by a green side salad peppered with watercress.*

**SERVES 3–6**

INGREDIENTS

*3 pink-skinned sweet potatoes, each weighing about 450 g/1 lb*
*salt*
*75 g/3 oz/6 tbsp butter, sliced*
*black, white and cayenne peppers*

2 ▲ The potatoes can either be served in halves or whole. For halves, split each one lengthways and make close diagonal cuts in the flesh of each half. Then spread with slices of butter, and work the butter and seasonings roughly into the cuts with a knife point.

3 ▲ Alternatively, make an incision along the length of each potato if they are to be served whole. Open them slightly and put in butter slices along the length, seasoning with salt and the peppers.

I ▲ Wash the potatoes, leaving the skins wet. Rub salt into the skins, prick them all over with a fork, and place on the middle shelf of the oven. Turn on the oven at 200°C/400°F/Gas 6 and bake for about an hour, until the flesh yields and feels soft when pressed.

**COOK'S TIP**

*Sweet potatoes cook more quickly than ordinary ones, and there is no need to preheat the oven.*

# Puddings

*The Louisiana tooth is very sweet, and Louisianans do like to end a meal with a proper pudding. For our tastes, something as sweet, spicy and substantial as their bread pudding is a good finish to a light meal of soup or a salad – but if it still defeats delicate appetites, the left-overs will be just as satisfying the next day. Sticky pies and sumptuous cakes, usually featuring the favourite pecan nuts, are more special desserts, and ice creams are particularly popular on summer days when the humidity, as well as the temperature, soars.*

# Bread Pudding with Cranberry Sauce

*A homely Louisiana classic that may be made more elegant with creamy or rum-flavoured sauces. I prefer the scarlet tartness of cranberries to offset such a sweet and substantial pudding.*

**SERVES 6–8**

INGREDIENTS

*50 g/2 oz/4 tbsp butter, melted*
*750 ml/1¼ pints/3 cups milk*
*3 eggs*
*100 g/3½ oz/½ cup caster sugar*
*1 tsp vanilla essence*
*2 tsp ground cinnamon*
*½ nutmeg*
*400 g/14 oz/9 cups cubed bread cut from a*
   *day-old French loaf (including crust)*
*50 g/2 oz/½ cup chopped walnut kernels*
*75 g/3 oz/½ cup sultanas*

**For the cranberry sauce**
*350 g/12 oz/3 cups cranberries, fresh or*
   *frozen*
*finely grated peel and juice of 1 large*
   *orange*
*25 g/1 oz/2 tbsp caster sugar*

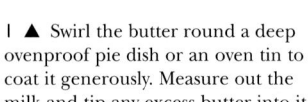

I  ▲ Swirl the butter round a deep ovenproof pie dish or an oven tin to coat it generously. Measure out the milk and tip any excess butter into it.

2  Beat the eggs with an electric whisk until light and frothy, then beat in the sugar, vanilla essence and cinnamon and grate in the nutmeg. Finally mix in the milk.

3  ▲ Pack the bread cubes into the pie dish, scattering the walnuts and sultanas among them as you go.

4  ▲ Pour the custard mix over slowly and evenly and leave to stand for 45 minutes, by which time only a little of the liquid should show round the rim.

5  Preheat the oven to 180°C/350°F/Gas 4. Bake the pudding in the oven for 45 minutes until risen and puffy, raising the heat to 200°C/400°F/Gas 6 for the last 10–15 minutes if it is not turning golden on top.

6  ▲ To make the cranberry sauce, put the berries into a saucepan with the orange peel and juice and the sugar.

7  ▲ Stir over a low heat until the sugar dissolves, then cook until the berries pop and the mixture thickens into a jam consistency. Serve hot or cold.

**COOK'S TIP**

*Left-overs of both the pudding and the sauce are good cold or reheated.*

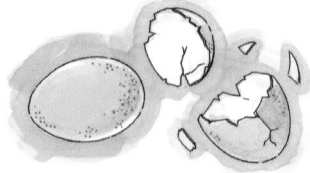

# Pecan Pie

*A favourite pie all over the southern states, where pecans flourish. Louisiana is no exception.*

**SERVES 6**

INGREDIENTS
**For the pastry**
*200 g/7 oz/1¾ cups plain flour*
*pinch of salt*
*115 g/4 oz/½ cup butter*
*dry pulses or rice for baking blind*

**For the filling**
*3 eggs*
*good pinch of salt*
*1 tsp vanilla essence*
*200 g/7 oz/¾ well-packed cup soft dark*
  *brown sugar*
*4 tbsp golden syrup or light corn syrup*
*50 g/2 oz/4 tbsp butter, melted*
*115 g/4 oz/1 cup chopped pecan kernels,*
  *plus 12 pecan halves*

**To serve**
*whipped cream or vanilla ice cream*

I ▲ Mix the flour with a pinch of salt, then rub in the butter with your fingertips to a coarse sand consistency. Add iced water a little at a time, mixing first with a fork, then with your hand, until the mixture gathers into a dough. Be mean with the water.

2 Wrap the dough in cling film and refrigerate for 30–40 minutes. Preheat the oven to 190°C/375°F/Gas 5 for 20 minutes before you bake the tart.

3 ▲ Grease a 20–23 cm/8–9 in loose-based flan tin. Roll out the pastry to line the tin, pressing it gently into place with your fingers.

4 ▲ Run the rolling pin over the top of the tin to sever the surplus pastry.

5.▲ Prick the pastry base and line with foil. Fill it with dry pulses or rice and bake blind for 15 minutes, then remove the foil and pulses and bake for a further 5 minutes. Take the pastry case from the oven and lower the oven heat to 180°C/350°F/Gas 4.

6 Meanwhile, to make the filling, beat the eggs lightly with the salt and vanilla essence, then beat in the sugar, syrup and melted butter. Finally mix in the chopped pecans.

7 ▲ Spread the mixture in the half-baked pastry case and bake for 15 minutes, then take it from the oven and stud with the pecan halves in a circle.

8 Return to the oven and bake for a further 20–25 minutes until a thin metal skewer pushed gently into the centre comes out clean, with no uncooked mixture attached.

9 Cool the pie for 10–15 minutes and serve it warm with whipped cream or a scoop of vanilla ice cream.

**COOK'S TIP**

*The corn syrup American cooks use in their pie filling is not widely available outside the USA. Substitute golden syrup. You can, however, find it in the larger department store food halls in major cities.*

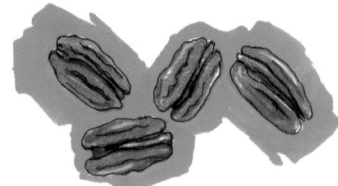

# Pralines

*Pronounced with a long 'a' and the stress on the first syllable, these resemble puddles of nut fudge more than the crisp biscuits Europeans think of as pralines. In Louisiana they are eaten as a dessert or whenever it seems a good idea to have something sweet with a cup of coffee.*

**MAKES ABOUT 30 PIECES**

INGREDIENTS

*225 g/8 oz/2 cups pecan halves*
*450 g/1 lb/2 well-packed cups soft light brown sugar*
*200 g/7 oz/1 cup white granulated sugar*
*300 ml/10 fl oz/1¼ cups double cream*
*175 ml/6 fl oz/¾ cup milk*
*1 tsp vanilla essence*

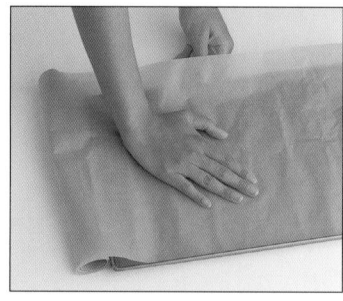

1 ▲ Roughly chop half the pecans and set all the nuts aside. Line 2–3 baking sheets with non-stick baking paper.

2 Stir the brown and white sugars, cream and milk together in a heavy-based saucepan over a medium heat. Stir continuously until the mixture reaches 119°C/238°F or the soft-ball stage (see Cook's Tip).

3 ▲ Remove from the heat immediately and beat with an electric beater or a balloon whisk until the mixture loses its sheen and becomes creamy in texture and grainy looking. This could take 15 minutes by hand or about 5 minutes with an electric beater.

4 ▲ Stir in the vanilla and both lots of nuts and drop tablespoons of the mixture onto the lined baking sheets, allowing it to spread of its own accord. Leave to cool and set at room temperature. Store between layers of greaseproof paper in a tight-lidded tin.

**COOK'S TIP**

*A mixture has reached the soft-ball stage when a teaspoonful dropped into cold water quickly sets to a soft ball. As this stage approaches, a spoonful of the mixture dribbled on the surface of the mixture in the pan will hold its trail. Test frequently towards the end of the cooking time unless you are using a sugar thermometer.*

# Bananas Foster

*A now-famous dessert named after Dick Foster, who was on the Vice Committee and therefore in charge of cleaning up the French Quarter of New Orleans in the 1950s.*

**SERVES 4**

INGREDIENTS

*75 g/3 oz/⅓ cup soft light brown sugar*
*½ tsp ground cinnamon*
*½ tsp grated nutmeg*
*50 g/2 oz/4 tbsp butter*
*4 tbsp banana liqueur*
*5 tbsp dark rum*
*4 firm bananas, peeled and halved*
*    lengthways*
*4 scoops firmly frozen vanilla ice cream*

**3 ▲** Add the bananas and heat through, turning to coat with the sauce.

**4** Tilt the pan if you are cooking over gas to set light to the sauce. If your stove is electric, light the sauce with a match. Hold the pan at arm's length while you do this.

**5** As soon as the flames die down, put 2 pieces of banana on each plate with a scoop of ice cream between them. Pour on the sauce and serve immediately.

I **▲** Mix the sugar, cinnamon and nutmeg together. Melt the butter in a heavy frying pan and add the sugar and spice mixture.

**2** Add the liqueur and rum and stir over the heat until the sauce is syrupy.

**COOK'S TIP**

*You can ring the changes with praline or walnut ice creams.*

# Coffee Ice Cream with Caramelized Pecans

**SERVES 4–6**

INGREDIENTS
**For the ice cream**
*300 ml/10 fl oz/1¼ cups milk*
*1 tbsp demerara sugar*
*25 g/1 oz/6 tbsp finely ground coffee or*
*  1 tbsp instant coffee granules*
*1 egg plus 2 yolks*
*300 ml/10 fl oz/1¼ cups double cream*
*1 tbsp caster sugar*

**For the pecans**
*115 g/4 oz/1 cup pecan halves*
*50 g/2 oz/4 tbsp soft dark brown sugar*

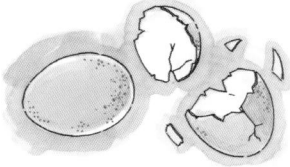

1 ▲ Heat the milk and demerara sugar to boiling point. Remove from the heat and sprinkle on the coffee. Leave to stand for 2 minutes, then stir, cover and cool.

2 In a heatproof bowl, beat the egg and extra yolks until thick and pale.

3 ▲ Strain the coffee mixture into a clean pan, heat to boiling point, then pour onto the eggs in a steady stream, beating hard all the time.

4 ▲ Set the bowl over a pan of gently simmering water and stir until it thickens. Cool, then chill in the fridge.

5 Whip the cream with the caster sugar. Fold it into the coffee custard and freeze in a covered container. Beat twice at hourly intervals, then leave to freeze firm.

6 To caramelize the nuts, preheat the oven to 180°C/350°F/Gas 4. Spread the nuts on a baking sheet in a single layer. Put them into the oven for 10–15 minutes to toast until they release their fragrance. Do not allow them to burn.

7 On top of the stove, dissolve the brown sugar in 2 tbsp water in a heavy pan, shaking it about over a low heat until the sugar dissolves completely and the syrup clears.

8 ▲ When the syrup begins to bubble, tip in the toasted pecans and cook for a minute or two over a medium heat until the syrup coats and clings to the nuts.

9 ▲ Spread the nuts on a lightly oiled baking sheet, separating them with the tip of a knife, and leave to cool. Store when cold in an airtight tin if they are not to be eaten on the same day.

10 Transfer the ice cream from the freezer to the fridge 30 minutes before scooping to serve, each portion topped with caramelized pecans.

**COOK'S TIP**

*You can serve good-quality bought ice cream with the same nutty garnish.*

# Watermelon Sherbet

*A pretty pink sherbet that makes a light and refreshing dessert, or that could appear before the main course to cleanse the palate at a grand dinner.*

**SERVES 6**

INGREDIENTS
*1 kg/2¼ lb piece watermelon*
*200 g/7 oz/1 cup caster sugar*
*juice of 1 lemon*
*2 egg whites*
*mint leaves to decorate*

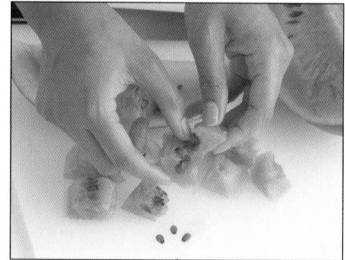

1 ▲ Cut the watermelon in wedges, then cut it away from the rind, cubing the flesh and picking out all the seeds.

2 ▲ Purée three-quarters of the flesh in a food processor or blender, but mash the last quarter on a plate – this will give the sherbet more texture.

3 Stir the sugar with the lemon juice and 120 ml/4 fl oz/½ cup cold water in a saucepan over very low heat until the sugar dissolves and the syrup clears.

4 ▲ Mix all the watermelon and the syrup in a large bowl and transfer to a freezer container.

5 Freeze for 1–1½ hours, until the edges begin to set. Beat the mixture, return to the freezer and freeze for a further 1 hour.

6 When the hour is up, whisk the egg whites to soft peaks. Beat the iced mixture again and fold in the egg whites. Return to the freezer for a further 1 hour, then beat once more and freeze firm.

7 Transfer the sherbet from the freezer to the fridge for 20–30 minutes before it is to be served. Serve in scoops, decorated with mint leaves.

# Creole Ambrosia

*A refreshing cold fruity pudding that can be made at any time of year.*

**SERVES 6**

INGREDIENTS
*6 oranges*
*1 coconut*
*25 g/1 oz/2 tbsp caster sugar*

**3** ▲ Peel the coconut with a sharp knife, then grate half the flesh coarsely, either on a hand grater or on the grating blade of a food processor.

**4** Layer the coconut and orange slices in a glass bowl, starting and finishing with the coconut. After each orange layer, sprinkle on a little sugar and pour over some of the reserved orange juice.

**5** Let the dessert stand for 2 hours before serving, either at room temperature or, in hot weather, keep it refrigerated.

**1** ▲ Peel the oranges removing all white pith, then slice thinly, picking out seeds with the point of a knife. Do this on a plate to catch the juice.

**2** ▲ Pierce the 'eyes' of the coconut and pour away the milk, then crack open the coconut with a hammer. (This is best done outside on a stone surface.)

**COOK'S TIP**

*Mangos instead of oranges make the dessert more exotic but less authentic.*

# Pecan Nut Divinity Cake

**SERVES 6–8**

INGREDIENTS
*275 g/10 oz/2½ cups pecan nuts*
*350 g/12 oz/3 cups plain flour*
*1½ tsp baking powder*
*½ tsp salt*
*225 g/8 oz/1 cup unsalted butter, at room*
*temperature*
*400 g/14 oz/2 cups caster sugar*
*5 eggs*
*225 ml/8 fl oz/1 cup milk*
*1 tsp vanilla essence*

**For the divinity icing**
*350 g/12 oz/3 cups icing sugar*
*3 egg whites, at room temperature*
*2 drops vanilla essence*

**1 ▲** Toast the pecans in batches in a heavy-based pan over a high heat, tossing regularly until they darken and give off a toasted aroma. Cool, then chop coarsely.

**2** Preheat the oven to 180°C/350°F/ Gas 4. Oil and lightly flour three 23 cm/ 9 in diameter cake tins. Sift the flour, baking powder and salt together. Toss half the pecans in 2 tbsp of the flour mixture. Reserve the remaining nuts for decoration.

**3 ▲** Cream the butter and caster sugar together until pale and fluffy and add the eggs, one at a time, beating well after each addition.

**4** Mix the milk with the vanilla essence. Stir the flour into the creamed mixture in 3 batches, alternating with the milk. Finally fold in the floured nuts.

**5** Pour the cake mixture into the prepared tins and bake in the oven for 30 minutes, until the tops are golden and the cakes have left the sides of the tins. Remove from the oven and leave to cool in the tins for 5 minutes before turning out onto racks to cool completely.

**6 ▲** To make the divinity icing, sift the icing sugar into a bowl, add the egg whites and set the bowl over a pan of boiling water. Whisk for 5–10 minutes until stiff peaks form.

**7 ▲** Add the vanilla essence. Remove the bowl from the pan and continue whisking for a further 2–3 minutes. Working very quickly, sandwich the cake layers together with some of the icing, sprinkling each layer with some of the reserved pecans.

**8 ▲** Ice the top and sides of the assembled cake and sprinkle the remaining nuts on top.

# Index